REMINISCENCES

OF

LIFE AND SPORT

IN

SOUTHERN INDIA

REMINISCENCES

OF

LIFE AND SPORT

IN

SOUTHERN INDIA

BY

COLONEL HEBER DRURY

GYAN

Published by

GYAN

Gyan Publishing House
5, Ansari Road
Daryaganj, New Delhi-110002
Phone: 011-47034999, 9811692060
E-mail: books@gyanbooks.com

Distribution Network
gyanbooks.com
India, USA, Canada, UK, Australia

ISBN: 978-81-212-5563-9 (HB)
First Published, 1890

2nd Impression 2024

Printed at: Gyan Press, Delhi.

REMINISCENCES OF LIFE AND SPORT IN SOUTHERN INDIA

Author: COLONEL HEBER DRURY

REMINISCENCES OF

LIFE AND SPORT IN SOUTHERN INDIA

REMINISCENCES

OF

LIFE AND SPORT

IN

SOUTHERN INDIA

BY

COLONEL HEBER DRURY

LATE MADRAS STAFF CORPS, AND ASSISTANT RESIDENT IN TRAVANCORE AND COCHIN

AUTHOR OF "THE USEFUL PLANTS OF INDIA," "HANDBOOK OF THE INDIAN FLORA," ETC. ETC.

"But tell me thine adventure; that will be
A joy to think of in long winter nights
When stormy billows make my lullaby."—SOUTHEY

LONDON

W. H. ALLEN & CO., 13, WATERLOO PLACE

PALL MALL, S.W.

1890

TO THE

REVD. B. H. DRURY,

PRESIDENT AND SENIOR FELLOW

OF

GONVILLE AND CAIUS COLLEGE, CAMBRIDGE,

THIS VOLUME IS DEDICATED

BY

HIS AFFECTIONATE BROTHER,

THE AUTHOR.

PREFACE.

IT may seem presumption in one whose acquaintance with India and its people only extended over a limited portion, and that chiefly in the South, to come forward as an author, when so many more gifted persons have written and are writing on subjects connected with the governing and governed classes. The younger Pliny in one of his letters quotes the dictum of his uncle, the naturalist, that no book was so bad, but that profit might be derived from some part of it. I take courage from this truism, and even if, as is most probable, the worthless far exceeds the good, yet I must throw myself on the clemency of my readers, and submit to the consequences. Without any pretension to grandeur of diction, I have put together, sometimes in the shape of narrative, and at others in extracts from my Journals, such incidents, albeit trivial, as happened to me during my varied career, together with occasional remarks and anecdotes of the people with whom I lived. In every country which, like India, may be considered in a transition state, where, in spite of many conflicting interests, intellectual improvement is advancing with rapid strides, and where Progress is the watchword of the masses, it necessarily follows that new ideas and forms of thought must penetrate and mould themselves in the minds of men who are accepting the benefits of educational reform. In this case a new type of civilisation is grafted upon the effete superstitions and ignorance of the past; and antiquated customs, however quaint and barbarous, get lost and forgotten in the march of improvement and change. To preserve the interesting records of habits fast passing away, is one of the objects aimed at in these pages. And thus I launch my boat to swim or sink in the stream.

H. D.

CROWBOROUGH,
August, 1889

CONTENTS.

CHAPTER V.

CHAPTER VI.

LIFE AND SPORT IN SOUTHERN INDIA.

CHAPTER I.

Description of the Country—Neilgherry Hills—Coimbatore—Journey to Cochin—Trichore.

DURING a prolonged residence in so interesting a country as India, it must of necessity follow that even the most careless observer has at times been stimulated by the novelty of his surroundings, by the diversity of the people, their customs and religions, so alien to European ideas and habits, to remark and ponder upon the varied scenes among which his destiny has thrown him. Few countries, perhaps, have gone through more startling changes during the last thirty or forty years than the Peninsula and Upper Provinces of Hindostan. Wherever

British influence has prevailed and spread the ægis of its protection over conquered or semi-conquered states, the germs of civilization have burst forth and in their fruit brought peace and happiness to thousands. There can be no hesitation in saying that the Mutiny in 1857,* terrible

* In making this passing allusion to the Mutinies, I cannot forbear inserting in this place a remarkable, yet ridiculous document in the shape of a proclamation which had no inconsiderable circulation in Travancore at that period, and of which I procured a copy with some difficulty. The native mind was in a very excited state, and rumours of the most exaggerated description were widely disseminated and in many instances as readily believed. Designing persons, ready at such times to work on the timid feelings of the lower and uneducated classes, invented and propagated a thousand falsehoods, hostile of course in their tendency to the British Government. The following *morceau*, the authenticity of which I can vouch for, was readily accepted and read by the ignorant natives, especially in the Eastern districts. It was not easy to trace the author of so mischievous a document, but it was believed to have been the production of a Syrian priest (a Cathanar), one of a numerous and turbulent race in those parts, often indulging in rancorous feelings towards the British :—

"Proclamation published by the Emperor of Russia, who has recently garrisoned Madras, for the information of his Highness the Rajah of Travancore, General Cullen, the British Resident, and also the following classes as it was in its temporary results, had the effect of clearing the political atmosphere, and evolving a more wholesome state of things through

of people—viz., Brahmins, Schetriahs, Chetties, Concanies, Europeans, East Indians, Scindians, Syrians, Roman Catholics, Mussulmans, Parsees, Jews.

"We hereby give below certain accounts at large we had touched on but briefly in our previous proclamation :—

"Subsequent to 984 the monarchy of the several states were for some time without a war. In 1029 the Emperor of Russia set out on a visit to the Patriarch of Antioch with all his Imperial suite. On his route he touched at Great Britain, an island belonging to the Turks and the Company. This island is surrounded by four rivers and extends from the German Ocean to Turkey. The population amounts to fifty crores and nine lakhs. The island is distinguished for a splendid palace occupied by the Company's sovereign, and a tent for the ladies. The country produces copper and iron, and its inhabitants are exempt from the distresses of poverty.

"The Company's regiments not only objected to the march of the Russian Emperor, but prevailed on his army to pay allegiance to them. This was communicated to the Commander-in-Chief of the Company's regiments, accompanied by a remonstrance against the conduct of the latter. He answered that he would withdraw all objections should his sovereign permit him. He accordingly brought the circumstance to the notice of his sovereign, when the latter ordered a force of the infidels the length and breadth of the country. The sincere and staunch attachment of native states to British rule and protectorate are daily acknowledged and increasing as years and events go on. Education is spreading in every direction and bearing fruit commensurate with the

to be collected. The movements of the enemy were perceived by the Russian Emperor from the summit of a hill, who immediately hastened to his capital. He had collected, in communication with his twenty-seven tributary chiefs, a force consisting of sixty-four regiments, and declared an open war at the foot of the mountain Keron (?). In the course of five hours he became master of London. There he had the curiosity to see a street of shoemakers as long as a four days' journey, and yielding a revenue of fifty crores and nine lakhs of rupees.

"We continued our march and conquered countries of forty-five days' journey. We duly fortified them and proceeded still further to the Himalayahs. We then made a treaty with the Company. There are many other particulars of still greater importance. In the course of the war a Subadar from each of the opposite forces was engaged in single combat. Although the hairs of the head of the combatant on our side were pulled out, yet he was not sensible of the same. They displayed extraordinary courage. We therefore conferred on each of them a public office and a salary of two thousand rupees.

"You will continue to communicate with me from time to time the particulars of your country!"

labour and expense necessarily involved in its introduction. The native mind is being stirred to its depths, and with laudable zeal and ambition, the higher classes especially, irrespective of creed or caste, are demanding a share in the government of the country. In a word, the future of India is the problem of the day.

And now, what is India like?—a question often put, but so difficult to answer, and about as puzzling as if the Emperor of China were to ask an Englishman, What is Europe like? It is a country comprising every description of climate, scenery, people, language and manners. Did any one who asked that short and simple question consider for one moment the vast system of our Indian Empire—its numerous races, divisions and religions? Its mixed populations, the castes, and all varying in language and character; the mild, the warlike, the savage and the civilized; the wealthy and enterprising Parsee, the educated Hindoos of Calcutta and Madras, the fierce and lawless Patan, the bloodthirsty Arab, the bigoted and crafty Brahmin, the superstitious pilgrim and deluded faqueer, and lastly the wild man of the woods. By such a diversity of races is this portion of God's fair earth inhabited, a motley collection of human beings scattered over the country included between the Himalayah and Cape Comorin, Scinde and the borders of the Chinese Empire. And such is denominated India, a term comprising more than is dreamt of in the philosophy of most inquirers, and a slight insight into whose history, either political, domestic, or historical, would stagger most minds, however eager for a knowledge of the social and moral relations of these remarkable races and the countries they inhabit.

These records, and the experiences I have undergone, have solely to do with the southern portions of the Peninsula, embracing both sides of the coast, the Malabar and the Coromandel; and from Bangalore to Cape Comorin there are few spots in the interior with which I have not at various intervals become more or less acquainted. In this small space no less than five distinct languages are spoken, and these over an area not more than six hundred miles in length, and three hundred in breadth. And then again how varied is the aspect of the country! In the province of Tanjore the eye ranges over a boundless extent of rice cultivation, stretching for miles and miles in every direction, with scarcely an elevated spot to break the monotony of the changeless scene. These rice-fields have bestowed on Tanjore the well-earned name of the "Granary of the East"; a few topes or groves of cocoa palms lie interspersed here and there between the open tracts of cultivation, giving shelter to a few occasional huts, the abodes of the labourer and his family. Villages, too, of various sizes and extent are met with, generally at the distance of eight or ten miles apart, but their confines are soon passed, and the traveller again gazes over the green unlimited tracts of paddy-fields.

Look now at the neighbouring district of Trichinopoly. Here, it is true, we meet with rice-fields in plenty, watered by the Cauvery and Coleroon rivers, but a greater part of the province consists of open sandy plains, presenting a more or less undulating surface in most parts, and bounded on its north frontier by hills whose height ranges from one to two thousand feet. Trichinopoly will be always associated with gold chains and cheroots, for both of which articles it is famous. In military annals, during the days of Clive and Lawrence, it will always hold a name. Much brisk fighting took place in the neighbourhood of the capital of the district between our handful of troops and the French and their natives allies, and three rocks immediately outside the present cantonment, the French Rock, the Sugar-loaf Rock, and the Golden or Fakeer's Rock, might tell of many a stern conflict fought beneath their heights in olden days. Some forty years ago, when I was in garrison there, there was a large wooden cage attached to a gibbet, which was fixed on the summit of the Sugar-loaf Rock, and inside the cage were the bones of a murderer, bleached white by exposure to the burning sun. They were those of a Sepoy who had deliberately shot a European officer. He who met with this unmerited fate was named Wahab, and had only been recently married. It was one morning when his regiment had assembled for ball-practice at the foot of this identical rock, that one of the men of his company stepped from the ranks and deliberately fired his musket at young Wahab. The wound proved mortal, and before ten o'clock the same morning he was a corpse. The Sepoy, on being questioned as to his reasons for committing so diabolical a deed, replied that he could not say why he did it, and declared that he was actuated by no revenge, either against that particular officer or any other. Often have I pondered over the untimely fate of that poor young man, as I myself have been at ball-practice beneath the rock, and gazing meditatively on the whitened bones as the creaking cage rocked to and fro with an unearthly noise in the howling wind. Nor is the Golden Rock without a similar tale of horror. Many years ago a trooper of a cavalry corps then stationed at Trichinopoly, impelled by some savage thirst for blood, drew the pistol from his holsters while on parade with his regiment, and fired at his commanding officer, wounding him severely in the arm. At that moment the adjutant, who was close by, rushed at the trooper to cut him down, but the latter instantly galloped off, and the adjutant after him in full chase. Away they both went through the cantonment, the trooper fast gaining ground, till some other English officers, who had observed the whole affair, had armed themselves with muskets and followed rapidly with the intention of avenging the dastardly attack upon the colonel. The trooper at last, getting clear of the cantonment, made straight away across the open plain towards the Golden Rock, his pursuers following at his heels. On the top of this rock is a Mahommedan shrine, which is held very sacred, and the trooper, who was a Mussulman, though he could not have hoped for refuge on this spot, yet imagined he might meet death better upon such holy ground. His fate was sealed, and he knew it. He scarcely reached the summit when an officer, who had dismounted, followed closely upon him, and levelling his musket shot him dead.

As a station for troops, Trichinopoly is exceedingly hot, but not unhealthy. This may be accounted for by the extreme openness of the surrounding country, one extensive plain of sand. Like most other places, however, it is subject to periodical visitations of cholera, at times very severe, and the last year I was there there were carried out of the fort not less on an average than one hundred corpses daily for several days.

To the north of Trichinopoly lies the district of Salem, from which it is separated by various ranges of hills, not of any considerable elevation. Such are the Putchah Mullays and the Koolay Mullays, or Hills of Death, the latter so called from the deadly fever which prevails there at all seasons of the year. Salem is a hilly district, and the Shevaroy Hills, at the foot of which the town of Salem is situated, are about 4,500 feet above the sea. The table-land on their summit affords a favourite resort for the European residents, who can enjoy a free and bracing climate, free from fever and other epidemics, and where, during the cold months, there is a slight frost in the early mornings. Large parts are planted with coffee, and these plantations are increasing every year. English fruits, too, and flowers flourish here excellently, and though game is not very abundant, yet woodcock are plentiful in the season, and elk, bison and tigers may frequently be met with in the interior. At the same time it cannot be denied that Salem itself is the very hot-bed of cholera. Here it was that Captain Bevan lost wife and children, his whole family, in three days, the one following the other in succession to the grave. The tombs in the churchyard will testify how many other young Englishmen have been cut off by the same fell disease in the prime of life. Yet I was here seven months on command, and although I had the melancholy task of following several of my dearest friends to their last home, still I liked the place in spite of such drawbacks, and formed there many strong friendships, unforgotten in after life.

Next in succession comes the district of Coimbatore; a fertile and well-populated province, within whose borders are the far-famed Neilgherry Hills, the grand sanitarium of India. Here in the space of a few hours you are transported from the burning plains of the Deccan to a climate resembling an English October—aye, and far colder in the months of January and February, when water is congealed to the thickness of one or more inches, and a white frost covers the ground every morning, with a piercing, chilling wind. It was about the year 1825 that a party of young civilians, while in pursuit of game, accidentally discovered this magnificent table-land. The past thirty years have done wonders towards the development of the natural resources and charms of this favoured region. An immense artificial lake has been formed in the centre of the principal station, and every elevated piece of ground around and on its banks has been adorned with beautiful villas and gardens. The lake is seven miles in circumference, and at the eastern end of it has sprung up a large native town, where shops full of every commodity, both European and Oriental, are to be found. The town of Ootacamund is on a table-land at the height of 7,500 feet above the sea; while Dodabetta, the highest peak, reaches an altitude of 9,000. Here the invalid finds himself almost as by magic wafted to his native climate and land, and with a brighter sun and clearer atmosphere than he finds withal under his own foggy and cloud-covered skies. Almost every description of fruit and flower grows in abundance and in charming variety, and these growing side by side with luxuriant tropical shrubs, combine a garden scene which may in vain be looked for in the chilly climate of Old England. The very hedges are composed of geraniums, which, with their dark red and white flowers blooming in endless profusion over the whole place, cannot fail to attract the attention of the visitor on his first introduction to these lovely hills. The gardens are laid out with English taste, and are fragrant with English flowers. The apple, the strawberry, the peach and plum equally thrive in this generous soil. The blackbird, robin, and tomtit enliven the shrubberies with their well-known notes, and often while sitting in an arbour of an evening and listening to the blackbird's song a thousand recollections of home were awakened within me. I have been carried back to the gardens of my own home in England, the rambles and pursuits of boyish days have been renewed in imagination once again. I have in those moments fancied myself again in my native haunts, and my sojourn in the East but a dream!

But before I quit the subject of the Neilgherry Hills, I must say one word about those remarkable relics of former ages, the "Cairns" and

"Barrows," which are so plentiful in the neighbourhood of Ootacamund. I am not, I must confess, antiquarian enough to deduce from any reasoning the fact of their being the works of an ancient Scythian race—a theory which has been advanced and supported upon very fair and substantial grounds by many scientists of the present day; but I am inclined, upon an impartial examination of the arguments brought forward in proof of this theory, to believe that they are monuments of a Celto-Scythian race, and that the present race of Todas, or, more properly, Thautawars, are their descendants, whose ancestors were driven from the plains to these mountains upon the invasion of the Hindoos from Egypt. I am not aware that I can add anything new to what has already been written about these people. Both men and women are endowed with handsome features, but are so excessively dirty both in habits and appearance that all ideas of the "noble savage" at once vanish on their close acquaintance. They wear a habit somewhat resembling the Roman toga, and their deep black hair falls in ringlets over their neck and shoulders. They are a purely pastoral race, and are peaceful and harmless in their manners. According to their own traditions, they were driven to these mountains by the persecutions of Ravana, the demon-king of Ceylon, who was in mythological story the possessor of Southern India. So, unlike all Indian tribes, they wear no kind of turban, and they account for this by saying they vowed they would never cover their heads till they had avenged themselves on their enemies. That they came from the low country there can be no doubt, for some of their customs, especially that of polyandry, peculiar also to the Nairs and Canarese of the Western coast, prove an early intercourse between these people. Their manners, customs, and religious ceremonies are so closely allied to the ancient Druids of Britain, that the most superficial observer must be forcibly struck with the resemblance, and also that they all originated from one common stock; the early Scythians being from habit a wandering nomadic race, pushing their invading hordes to the remotest corners of the earth.

On these hills we find the aborigines an

almost perfect type of the ancient Briton. Their temples are built in exactly the same manner, circular with double rings of stones, and the spot chosen is in the midst of a thick wood or grove. The ceremonies observed at the religious festivals are similar also; in both cases a thick grove is selected, and a calf (or among the Druids, a bull) brought for the sacrifice. The officiating priest, first addressing the people, cuts a branch from the sacred tree, and then proceeds to sacrifice the victim. Again, an ancient Celtic house and what is called a Toda "Dairy" of the present day, are precisely similar in their construction, a square building with a conical roof surrounded by a low wall with one narrow entrance. Inside this Dairy is their altar and idol, merely consisting of an upright stone. This single stone was also the object of Druidical worship. At one spot, known as "Fair Lawn," there is the site of an ancient fortification, the foundations being clearly traceable; the ruins of buildings, the formation of streets, and remains of temples being easily recognized amid the surrounding heaps of earth under which they are buried. It has been suggested that this was the ancient chief town of the inhabitants. The Todas are not the only tribe that occupy these regions. I believe there are four or five others altogether. There are the Coorambas, a far more wild race than the former. They live in a much more secluded and wretched manner, without the slightest trace of civilization or even religion, and yet, curiously enough, the other tribes have a certain kind of awe and respect for these Coorambas, and believe them to be descendants of a far more ancient race, who erected the Cairns and Cromlechs found not only on these mountains, but on all high lands in Southern India, identical in form with those found in Europe and in England.

But my residence on these delightful hills was destined to be of short duration. My goal was Travancore, in the southernmost part of the Peninsula, and I commenced at once to arrange my plans for proceeding to that distant station. Leaving Conoor after an early breakfast I began to descend the pass leading into the low country. The scenery here is singularly wild and grand. On the left hand is a mountain rocky barrier covered with jungle and forest, and peaks of loftier hills stretching beyond, while on the right is a deep precipitous gorge overgrown with dense vegetation, beneath whose interlaced foliage you can distinctly hear the rushing waters of a mountain torrent as it flows rapidly over the rocky bed in its onward course, of which you can occasionally gain glimpses through breaks in the jungle. This vale is of no great width, for the opposite mountain rises immediately in an almost perpendicular direction, and is covered from the very summit with a thick and almost impervious forest, forming a most sublime and impressive scene. At intervals, at some slight turning of the road, an opening through the trees enables the traveller to command a most extensive prospect of the low country, stretching for forty or fifty miles away, and presenting the appearance of a scorched, burnt and parched plain, dotted here and there with a few low hills, and inconsiderable sheets of water. And this aspect is a representation of the truth, for most assuredly the sun uses its fiery strength over all this part of the country, and any one arriving from the green and smiling aspect of the hills will observe a strange contrast in the drear and desert plains of the lower lands. During this part of my journey I met scarcely any one save a few natives driving their oxen laden with supplies for the markets of Conoor or Ootacamund, while every half-hour the increase of a warmer atmosphere became sensible, till eventually I reached the bottom of the pass. A further ride of five miles brought me to the halting-place of Matypollium. As I had no servants and no bedding or luggage, I set to work to prepare as soft a couch as the materials at hand would admit of, and with my coat and trousers, a pair of boots, and a towel or two, I succeeded in making a tolerably comfortable pillow, and as fatigue is a wonderful assistant in smoothing down difficulties, I was soon reposing on a bed equal in comfort, for all that I could perceive, to the downiest couch in damask or velvet ever sought by the most luxurious Sultana of the East.

There is a legend attached to this part of the country which I will here relate. From the vast quantity of jungle that covers the base of these mountains, there is at times a feverish atmosphere lurking about, which proves fatal to those who attempt to pass a night under its deadly influence. It is thus accounted for by the natives : On the summit of the huge rock overlooking Matypollium there was formerly a castle inhabited by a giant called Pakasooren, who levied a tribute of a cart-load of provisions every day from the country people, and which enormous supply he first devoured and then devoured the driver; after which he gave the cart a kick, sending it thus ungraciously back for the purpose of being refilled on the morrow. In those days there was a large town called Moonoor-munglum on the other side of the river opposite to Matypollium, and here happened to arrive one day a Hindoo king, and on hearing of the exploits of this giant he resolved to fill the next cart-load of provisions and convey it himself to the ogre. However, getting hungry on the road he ate up all the supplies himself, and substituting a load of mud in their place, he drove up to the giant's castle. The latter, seeing the trick that had been played upon him, attempted to slay the king, upon which a fierce contest arose between them, in which the king was victorious, but, in dying, the giant pronounced a curse upon all that part of the country which was overshadowed by his mountain, saying it should be for ever afflicted with a pestilential fever. *Hinc illæ lacrymæ!*

What early risers we are or ought to be in India. How many people, I venture to ask, save labourers and travellers, ever see the sun rise in England from one year's end to the other? Few, if any, save by necessity or compulsion. Yet it is healthy and classical to rise betimes. Homer was an early riser, so was Virgil. So was our old friend the Eton Latin Grammar, who said "Surgere diliculo saluberrimum est,"—Let us hope he practised what he preached. I must own that it is not a very agreeable duty to rise some three or four hours before sunrise, and trudge along at a snail's gallop in rear of a marching regiment over a blind road, your horse and yourself nodding in sleep and in ill-humour at being roused up in abnormal hours. A little previous to daylight is, I think, the best time, so that when your nag is ready at the door you may be able to distinguish between a pig and plantain-tree, and avoid knocking your head against either. Such was the hour of dawn when I set off this morning, the road rough and stony, almost blocked by prostrate boulders, and proving by the constant trippings of the horse what a feast of specimens lay here for the geologist, who might work and collect here to his greatest satisfaction. So onwards I rode, till about eight o'clock it began to wax very warm, and, alas! I had no prospect of a breakfast before me, and only a very indistinct shadow of one behind me; for when I had started I had wrapped up a cold fowl, a biscuit or two, and a piece of cold mutton, and summoning a black little wretch of a boy from the village, had ordered him under threat of immediate chastisement to run as fast as his little dirty feet could carry him to the next bungalow, only twelve miles, a mere step for the lad, who had moreover the promise of threepence held out to him as a douceur at the end of his journey, so he could hardly complain. Away he started—the young Barnaby—but, of course, I overtook him before I had gone a mile, and I now amused myself with conjecturing about the time of day he would probably arrive. I myself reached my destination at half-past eight, and ordering milk from the village, I sat down to muse on the uncertainty, not of human life, but of our daily bread. How eagerly I watched and gazed through the trees for the faintest glimpse of that little urchin, who had all that was most valuable to me at that moment! At last, to my unspeakable joy, he hove in sight about eleven o'clock. *Oh! gaudia quanta fuerunt;* I set to with a degree of cannibalistic ardour that would make me ashamed to look a sheep or fowl in the face again. The attendant at the bungalow brought the milk, I drank it out of their black earthenware vessel, asking no questions. I had some brandy. They brought me a tin vessel, and diluting the former with water I drank, asking no questions, for to know the antecedent histories of the black vessel and the tin mug would have been a painful revelation of all that is dreadful. I know I breakfasted "full of horrors."

Little advantage could be gained by remaining in this hot and comfortless bungalow, so about two o'clock I set off under a broiling sun to ride twelve miles, to Coimbatore, which I reached about four. It was some time before I could ascertain where the public bungalow was, and asking your way to any place from a native is about as useful as addressing yourself to a post. "Ugh," "ow," "Iyoo," "oo"—and such like bearish ejaculations is all you can get from them. The most effectual way of making one of these stolid gentry of any possible utility is to commence with a not ungentle thrust at him to bring him first to his senses, and then force him onwards in front of you with a further supply of the *argumentum ad baculum*, mildly, of course, but effectively. I have known them to become very tractable, if not positively useful, under this treatment. After a good deal of dodging about the roads and turnings, the bungalow at last came in view, and to my dismay I found it after all to be occupied. *Que faire?* Happily one of the occupants turned out to be an old friend, Captain D——, who was en route to Trichinopoly. This cleared away all prospective difficulty in the matter of lodgings. Certainly, the mode of travelling and selection of vehicles has not reached its climax in this country. We must for many a long day be content with the snail's pace of ten miles an hour *per diem*, or thirty-five ditto *per noctem*, in a palanquin. Take which you choose, they are equally tiring and distressingly slow. The one makes you sleep all day, and the other prevents your sleeping all night. There appears to be no coming improvement either. Horses will not go faster in the next century than they do in this, and one can hardly suppose that the bearers will be able to boast of any physical improvement in the muscles of their legs in any future time. The spirit of old Weller does not live in the East, the roads oppose an insuperable obstacle to any kind of coachifying, and I should not wonder after all if, to use a school expression, we took a "double remove," and jumped from palanquins to railways at one bound, leaving the present generation of Hindoos in utter ignorance of the mail coach. In the meantime one would imagine that every one, even for individual and personal comfort, would exert himself to render the rate of travelling more speedy, and the manner of accomplishing it invested with more *agrémens* than it is at present accomplished withal; but somehow, looking at my friend D.'s primitive conveyance, I certainly considered that he had retrograded in the great question of locomotion. A large cart on two wheels, arched over with a matted covering and drawn by two bullocks, was the vehicle he had provided. It was one of the common carts of the country, the rate of travelling being about two miles an hour. Of course there are no springs, and every rut, stone, or hollow, *tells* upon the poor inmates. A blackee sits on the inner extremity of the pole to push and drive the oxen by twisting their long tails. On inspection I found that D. had, at any rate, not been wholly inattentive to his creature comforts, so sincerely wishing my friend as few joltings as possible, I bade him a hearty good night and farewell.

My next route was through a dense jungle, with occasional breaks displaying some charming wild scenery, the trees being of an enormous size, and the lovely and graceful bamboo spreading in masses in every direction. Apart from the peculiarities of tropical foliage, the landscape in its general features appeared to resemble a nobleman's park in England. Would I might follow up the simile, and record how I arrived at a nobleman's seat! Far, far from such luxury was the hovel I arrived at, and where I was fated to spend a long and weary day. A small space had been to all appearance purposely cleared in the dense jungle for the building of a few huts which, I concluded, formed the village, but which with great truth might be called a nest of thieves. Most unprepossessing was the exterior of a miserable house of rest for travellers, and the interior apartments were in true keeping with its outward features. Of all dirty, filthy cabins it was ever my lot to enter, this I think was the very worst. Certainly there was a table and a chair, so it was possible to sit down, but from their appearance they must have been there from immemorial times. The place was called Walliar. On approaching the door a black-looking ragamuffin accosted me with a salaam, whom I questioned summarily as to his immediate calling in respect to this so-called bungalow. "I am the thief, sir, attached to this bungalow, to take care of it," he replied in his own language. And a very capital thief you make, I thought, though I fear the nakedness of the land hereabouts prevents your following a very brisk trade in your special department. Well, I walked inside, and the thief walked out, and the whole day I watched him prowling about the house as if his existence depended on the safety of the household furniture aforesaid. Ah! it was a dreary day that! Wrapped in a towel, I had brought with me a fowl, a bunch of plantains, and a few potatoes, and on these I fed for breakfast and luncheon, and at last I mounted my horse and made a push for Palghaut, a further distance of fourteen miles. Arrived here I found my stock of provisions exhausted save one crust of bread, which I had carefully put by after my last meal at Walliar. Imagine then my delight at finding that my servants had been here about three o'clock in the afternoon with my luggage, and had departed again, leaving behind a couple of biscuits and a bottle of soda-water!

While I was making the best I could of this scanty but welcome meal, I chanced to take up the "Travellers' Book," and my eyes lit upon the following remark recorded therein :—"There is a butler attached to this bungalow who can provide all strangers with a chop or a cutlet at a very short notice." Dashing the book on the floor, I cried out for this noble fellow who undertook to supply a famished traveller with a "sudden surprise" at a moment's warning.*

A thousand blessings on the head of that kind and confiding traveller who so unconsciously bestowed this gratuitous information by which I benefited so largely. Not only chops and cutlets, but tea, muffins and bread, and all the more welcome as they were so unexpected. To encourage this worthy

* To the uninitiated I must explain that a "sudden surprise" is a common term for a fowl which, on the arrival of a traveller at a public bungalow is suddenly surprised in a very ungracious manner by the servants of the establishment, who with numerous sticks and stones and any handy missiles hunt the first victim they come across to death, and cook it on the spot. It is sometimes called a "sudden death," and is usually served up as a very tough gull.

factotum in his worthy vocation of butler and general provider, I rewarded him handsomely, far beyond the actual cost of the articles, for he deserved his reward, and others may possibly reap the profit. *Haud ignara mali*, &c. Again I patched up a pillow composed of the incongruous medley of boots, towels, and shooting-coats, and stretching myself on the rotten bedstead, was soon fast asleep, though terribly pestered by the mosquitoes.

The next morning I was up and off long before daybreak, and when the first streaks of dawn were just beginning to peep over the long range of mountains to the eastward, to my great disgust I overtook my servants, who ought to have been far in advance towards the next stage, from which we were now distant about twelve miles. Farewell all hopes of a breakfast that morning. But I had to push on, if only to reach shelter before the sun's rays were too powerful.

Next morning, about 8 A.M., I reached the miserable village of Putticaud, lying among hills, and built on a space redeemed from the surrounding jungle. A dirty shed was the best accommodation, and thankful was I even for that shelter. As I knew this locality to be famous for sport, especially large game, I summoned the head Shikaree, named Chundroyen, and inquired if any shooting was to be had in the neighbourhood. His reply was decidedly in the affirmative ; so about eleven o'clock he made his appearance with about seven or eight of his brethren in arms, each of whom had a matchlock and large knife, all weapons of a very primitive make and origin. They seemed very eager for the sport, though one or two were quite old men with grey hair and whiskers, and others boys of seventeen or eighteen. Shouldering my largest gun, we penetrated at once into the forest. We were soon marked as intruders by the crowds of monkeys, who, alarmed at our approach, were chattering among the high trees and leaping from branch to branch with wonderful agility, every now and then stopping to peep out from some opening in the foliage, as much as to say what business have you here ? Every now and then some large bird, as the toucan, would break forth from his hiding-place and, uttering a harsh, discordant scream, be quickly lost to sight and hearing; while on every side, amid their thick, leafy shelters, innumerable insects filled the air with a most inharmonious concert of hisses and cries. Treading softly over the dried leaves and branches that lay scattered along our path, we crept along in Indian file till we reached a large tree, and here my guides held a council of war, arguing at a fine rate for about a quarter of an hour. At the conclusion of this parley they motioned me to proceed onwards, and I had scarcely gone a couple of hundred yards when a loud stampede of some large animals a short way to my right hand made me instinctively cock my gun and prepare to fire.

"Bisons! bisons!" whispered my guide; "but they're gone."

I instantly darted into the jungle in hopes of getting a shot at them, but in vain; but my guide encouraged me by saying, "They are not far off, and we must get round them. We are certain of finding them."

One of the guides stayed with me and all the others went off and were soon out of sight. Following this old man, I came to the banks of a river, where the jungle became so dense that it was with the greatest difficulty we could force a passage through it. With the help of a large knife we cleared away the larger branches of brambles that obstructed our path, and creeping at times on hands and knees managed to make good our progress, slow but sure. Suddenly we came upon the fresh tracts of bison. Such good omens gave me fresh spirit, and although the incessant bending down was very fatiguing, I pushed on with much perseverance and some hope. At last we emerged into an open space, and my guide cautioning me to be very silent, told me to take up a position behind a large tree near which I was standing. Here I remained with breathless anxiety waiting for some animal to rush out of his lair, and I had not long to remain in this suspense, for in a few moments I indistinctly heard a rustling of the bushes, from which I was sure something was approaching. And it was coming from the very path from which I had issued from the thicket. Oh! the excitement of that moment, those know too well, what words cannot express, who have felt the coming of the game.

Suddenly I descried an enormous dark mass of some object slowly advancing towards me. My guide touched me and made a sign. I raised my finger in acknowledgment of his caution. Then came out the noble beast and stood before me, not fifteen yards off. It was a huge bull bison. He paused and sniffed the air, evidently having smelt treachery. Still he advanced a few more paces, and again paused. I levelled my gun and fired. Stunned by the shock he fell to the ground, and I thought my prey secure; but to my great mortification the animal rose again, and with a snort that made the wood echo, he dashed through the jungle and was immediately out of sight. For two reasons I regretted the loss of my game. No sportsman likes to return home with an empty bag, and I left a wounded animal to die, perhaps in agony of pain. I gave up all chase after following his tracks for a short distance, the natives assuring me they should find him dead the next day. To follow up a wounded bison is extremely dangerous. They lie in wait for their pursuers and, enraged with pain, rush furiously out of the bushes in which they lie concealed. Whether the animal was found or not I never ascertained, for, a disappointed hero, I left the same evening for the next station of Trichore, about nine miles distant.

The Residency at Trichore is charmingly situated, and the view around is singularly beautiful. The eye ranges over a vast extent of well-wooded hill and dale, and the distant mountains, covered with dense forests, stretch far away in the distance, lending that enchantment to the view which the admirer of nature so much enjoys. At this place there is a celebrated pagoda of great sanctity. Europeans are not permitted to enter its sacred precincts, and none but the purest Brahmins its Holy of Holies inside. When Tippoo came this way he soon sent the Brahmins to the right about, for he let his rabble soldiery loose upon the temple, seized the treasures, and forced the Hindoos to become followers of Mahomedanism. Never was such a complete turnout as that old tyrant made at this shrine. Time, however, has restored the priests again to their national worship, and years and money have partially effaced the pollution of Tippoo and his myrmidons. A considerable portion of the population here are Christians, belonging to the Romo-Syrian branch, of which so many converts are scattered throughout Malabar and Travancore. Latterly, a Protestant mission has been established here, unhappily giving rise to much violent altercation between the rival sects. On one occasion the parties came to blows, and so angry and excited were the pugilists that one of the Romo-Syrians lost part of his nose in the scuffle. His adversary certainly chose a tender part, and I hope was satisfied with his mouthful. About twenty-four miles from Trichore is Currapudnum, where there is a bungalow built upon a high open spot looking down upon the backwater, which said backwater is a large inlet from the sea, stretching from Chowghaut to Trevandrum, a course of nearly two hundred miles, the receptacle of numerous rivers and streams that rise in the Western Ghauts, and affording an interior water communication of great import to the Cochin and Travancore countries. The armlets and creeks of this vast inland lake are very beneficial to cultivation in places where the salt waters are excluded. Rice-fields are everywhere abundant. At one season the ground is covered with cultivation, and then, as the monsoon approaches, the whole becomes an extensive surface of water, and what before were smiling fields, now become one immense lake, filled with aquatic birds, and boats and canoes gliding in all directions over its surface.

I here found one of the Residency boats in attendance to convey me to Cochin, and as soon as my servants and baggage arrived, I embarked and bore away for the latter place. The boat was most comfortably fitted up. The interior was lined with cushions, and on the top outside was a sofa, where one could recline in the evening after the sun had gone down. The crew consisted of a steersman and fourteen rowers. The Union Jack was flying at the stern, and to the tune of a merry song we dashed rapidly through the waters like a "thing of life." It was near midnight when I reached Cochin. Not a soul was moving in the streets, nor could I find any one who could tell me where lived the doctor to whose house I wanted to go. The only person apparently awake in the whole town was the sentry at the guard-house, and as I saw his dim form at a distance by the feeble light of an oil lamp, I hastened up to him to make inquiries, when he immediately pointed out the house I required to find. However, I was not soon admitted after all my rovings about. The occupant was evidently wrapt in a deep sleep, and after vain and fruitless thumpings and knockings at his door for more than half an hour I was nearly giving it up in despair, and going to return to the boat and sleep there till morning. At last I hit upon the following expedient. I conceived the idea of hoisting up one of the boatmen on the garden wall, and letting him drop down on the other side, whence he could make his way and rouse up the inmates. The fall I calculated could not be very great. With considerable reluctance the fellow scrambled up with assistance, and letting himself down the length of his body clung to the wall with his hands, and cried out to be lifted up again, as there was no bottom. "It's all right," I cried out; "let go, drop," and disengaging his fingers from their hold I deprived him of all support, and down he went. There was a faint "ugh!" as he alighted at the bottom, but he was not hurt, and he went at once, roused up the establishment, and I soon got housed for the night. The doctor. who came to meet me in his night habille, said, "Why, how did you get in?" "Dropped a boatman from the outer wall into the garden," was my curt reply. "Dropped him!" said the doctor in mute astonishment, "why, there's a large gutter underneath. Is the man hurt?" "Not a bit," I said; "I believe it took away his breath, nothing more." The next morning we went to see the gutter. Poor man! He might have made a bad job of it. "But, doctor," I said, "how is it you did not hear me knocking? It was surely loud enough." "Hear you! I should think I did. I thought I should never get to sleep." "Then why didn't you open the door?" "Because I thought it was the undertaker. Next door to me lives a coffin-maker, and every night he hammers and hammers away at his trade. When I heard you knock, I thought it was the old fellow again at his work, and muttered to myself, confound the fellow, there he goes at his coffins again. I wish people wouldn't die so fast, and give less work to my industrious neighbour." I was glad to find my room was at the other side of the house, and that I could rest quietly without being disturbed by dreams of being nailed up in my coffin like my poor friend.

CHAPTER II.

Cochin—Relics of the Portuguese—Jews, white and black — Christian sects — Quilon — Courtallum — Elephant shooting.

COCHIN is a singular place, take it all in all, full of quiet streets and quaint houses. It has a complexion peculiarly its own, neither wholly Portuguese, Dutch, or English, but a mixture of all three nationalities. I believe the town can boast of more accumulated filth and poverty than any other town of its size and character in this part of the world. At fitful intervals there has been a considerable amount of trade and commercial activity here, and ship-building has always been carried on to a great extent. The dangerous character of the bar, however, at the entrance of the river, and the shallowness of the river itself has always proved a great obstacle to its increasing prosperity in this line. No vessel drawing more than eleven feet can cross the bar at high tide. For cheapness of living Cochin is, or used to be, unrivalled, and consequently is resorted to by numerous pensioners, chiefly English, for natives detest the place. There are also many old resident Dutch families, as well as descendants of the Portuguese. The chief article of food consists of poultry, all kinds of which are bred here in great quantities. Ducks at the time I am speaking of were four shillings a dozen. Fowls might almost be had for the asking, while geese and turkeys were in proportion exceptionally cheap. But there is one great deficiency. There is no drinking water, save what is very brackish and bad. Government provides a boat to bring fresh water for those who choose to pay for the luxury, from a distance of fourteen miles, a certain quantity being given gratuitously to the officials. The poorer inhabitants are forced to drink the brackish water, which is known to engender that horrible disease "Elephantiasis." I do not exaggerate when I say, that on an average one person in every fifteen or twenty of the population is either affected with this complaint, or with actual leprosy, and the frightful objects which are constantly met at every corner of the streets testify to the prevalence of the scourge, and have no parallel, I am convinced, in any part of the world.

This town is the capital of the principality of the same name. In the Malyala language—(the language spoken in these parts)—it is called "Cocci," deriving its name from a small river which empties itself there into the sea. That part of the coast has undergone considerable physical changes within the memory of man. Old prints show the Portuguese and Dutch ports half a mile or more out into the sea compared with the present outer sea-wall. In 1341, the sea threw up the Island of Vaipeen, on the north side of Cochin. The waters breaking through the banks of the river Cocci, swept away the village and formed a larger river and backwater, and so spacious a harbour that ships of considerable tonnage can lie securely at anchor in the river, on the N.E. side of the town. This island is three miles long and about one mile broad. In the native language it is called "Poodooveypa," from

Poodoo new, and *Veypa* foundation, and the people date their era from the period of its origin. The town of Cochin was built by the Portuguese in the tenth year after the arrival of Vasco de Gama at Calicut. It was greatly improved by Francisco and Alphonso Alberquerque, in 1504, and soon became one of the wealthiest commercial towns in these parts. The Dutch, who wrested nearly all the important Settlements from the Portuguese, soon had an eye to Cochin, and attacked and took it in 1663. Probably in its palmiest days it was a thriving, busy place, but in extent, and consequently in wealth and prosperity, it could only progress to a certain limit, owing to its being surrounded so much by water on one side, and the native territory closing it in on the other. The streets are tolerably regular. On first entering the old-fashioned houses you mount a flight of steps to the dwelling-rooms, the so-called ground-floors having been formerly used for stores or slaves, or both, but converted by the modern occupants into stables, a very inconvenient arrangement, but unavoidable, for the savoury odour of such a neighbourhood is not pleasant in a drawing-room.

The descendants of old Dutch and Portuguese families are very numerous here, and the latter especially still retain the names of the best aristocratic families of Portugal. None of them are of pure descent, with the exception of a few among the Dutch, who can still boast of a pedigree untainted by any admixture of native blood. The rest are all half-castes with the sounding names of De Silva, Rodriquez, Pinto, Gomez, and so on. The numbers who compose this *tiers état* in the heterogeneous population of Cochin are very considerable. They used formerly to be called "Topasses," from a singular derivation, *Tu Pai* (thou boy), in Portuguese. The latter people having taught their language to the slaves born in their houses, made use of them as interpreters in dealing with the natives, and used to say, *Tu pai, falla aquel,* "You boy, say so and so." The term Topass has now fallen into disuse, but, curious enough, the Europeans in India invariably call out "Boy" (Pai) whenever they require their servant, East Indian or native. I have read other accounts where the word is derived from Sanscrit, *Dui,* signifying "two," and *Bashi*, a man speaking two languages, an interpreter. The French called them *Gens de Chapeau*, because they wore a *Topie* or small hat in contradistinction to the turbaned natives. But in whatever liberty the Topasses might indulge with regard to hats, there was in early days a rule that none of them might wear shoes or stockings, except by paying for the privilege of so doing. They were obliged to pay a similar tax for carrying a cane, but these rules have long been discontinued. They have several customs peculiar to themselves which, as they are not observable among other castes, they have probably adopted from their Portuguese ancestors. They consider it particularly unlucky if, on the birth of a child, some one does not constantly keep singing to the new-born infant. When man and wife go out together they never walk side by side as we do, but the husband walks first and the wife follows. When mourning for a deceased relative they wear their black coats inside out, and let their beards grow. This latter is a native custom. But upon the whole, proud and idle as they are, they have many useful qualities. As writers and accountants they are constantly employed in English offices and merchant houses. They follow various trades among themselves, but seldom grow wealthy owing to one failing, that they spend their money as fast as they make it, their principal ambition being to vie with the European gentleman in all the finery and luxury of polished life.

In writing about Cochin I must not omit to say a few words on the colony of White Jews occupying one of the lower suburbs, apart and distinct from the other inhabitants. They have been dwelling here for many generations. The part where they reside is called Jews-town, and this contains in all about one hundred families, and even these are fast decreasing by death or emigration, for many have already returned to Jerusalem, which is apparently the main object of them all when their poverty does not forbid them, for they are poor beyond belief. They are remarkably fair, and some of the women are beautiful, with long light ringlets and blue eyes. It was in the year 68 A.D. that 10,000 Jews with their families came to the coast of Malabar, and spread themselves over various places, chiefly on the sea-coast. It was not until the arrival of the Portuguese in the fifteenth century that they still further spread themselves, and in consequence of meeting with great oppression, soon found their way as far south as Cochin, where they obtained a grant of land from the reigning Rajah, and which they have held ever since. This was about A.D. 1560. There are besides these many Black Jews, so called in contradistinction to the others, and these are far more numerous throughout the whole of the western coast. They are converts formerly made by the White Jews. Throughout this part of India there are many Christian sects, chiefly Nestorians and Romo-Syrians, descendants of the early converts of the Portuguese, and even long anterior to that time by the Apostle St. Thomas himself, who is said to have come to India A.D. 52, and who was buried at what is now called St. Thomas's Mount, about eight miles from Madras. The town of St. Thomé also on the coast, five miles from Madras, bears testimony to his mssion to these countries. The sect of Nestorians arose in the fifth century, their founder being a Syrian bishop of Constantinople. In the year 485 they obtained a footing in Persia under their leader Barsumas, and from thence spread into almost every country of the East. The Nestorians on the coast of Malabar are called the Christians of St. Thomas. It must be recollected that theirs is quite an independent Church, and disclaims all connection with the Papal Church and its teachings. Not so the Romo-Syrians, who are here also a numerous body. Their conversion to Popery dates back about three centuries, effected by the priests of Aleppo. In Malabar and Travancore they number about 200,000 souls.

"It is probable," writes Fra Bartolomeo, who travelled in these parts about a hundred years ago, "that a great part of the Christians of St. Thomas in India came from Persia or Chaldea. The rites, liturgy, ceremonies and books of these Christians bear evident marks of a Chaldaic or Persian extraction. Though the Malabar dialect is at present the mother tongue of the Christians of St. Thomas in

India, they, however, employ Chaldaic phrases when they speak of sacred or religious objects It is, therefore, not improbable that a considerable number of Christians went from Persia and Chaldea to India, and united themselves to the small body of the original Indian Christians, whose ancestors were formerly converted to the Christian faith by the Apostle Thomas at Maliapour, which they unanimously consider as the place that first gave birth to Christianity in India. Thus much is certain, that all these Christians in the year 1502, at which period Vasco de Gama came a second time to Malabar, were Nestorians. Some of them denied the divinity of Christ, and could not endure images; but, on the other hand, they showed a greater reverence for the Holy Cross. They had no other sacraments but Baptism, Communion, and the consecration of priests. They believed that the souls of the Just were not admitted into the presence of God before the final judgment, and that till that period they were to remain in Eden. In the year 1599 these Christians were united to the Catholic Church, from which, however, they afterwards separated in 1653."

In addition to the above interesting remarks on the Syrian Communities and their tenets, a remarkable account of the origin and spread of Christianity in Malabar was written in the Syriac language, and was in possession of one of their bishops. The title ran thus: "The antiquity of the Syrian Christians, and historical events relating to them." I give the following extract from what must be a curious document:

"Fifty-two years after the birth of the Messiah, the Holy Apostle Thomas arrived at Maliapour, on the Coromandel coast, preaching the Gospel and founding Churches there. Passing from thence to Malabar, the holy man landed on the coast of Maliankurray (situated between Cranganoor and Paroe), preached and taught, and built Churches in that island; and having finished his work in these parts and ordained two priests, returned to the land of the Pandies (as the natives of Coromandel are called) to teach the people there. But whilst he was thus occupied, the Apostle was pierced by the heathens with spears, and thus ended his life."*

* The reader of Gibbon will find an account of the

Fra Bartolomeo reckons the number of Roman Catholics in his days in Malabar at 100,000, and alludes to conversion as progressing most rapidly. In two years (1780–81) he confirmed about 20,000 persons. In the census taken in 1854, there were 81,886 Romo-Syrians, 109,123 Syrians, 1,737 East Indians in Travancore alone. But these figures can hardly be depended upon as giving a very correct return of native converts. The Syrians, it will be observed, are the most numerous. Their history is full of interest. Impatient of control or amalgamation with other Christian sects, they possess, with all their ignorance and obduracy, a monument of vitality and progress strangely in contrast with other sects. Roman Catholics have failed to bring them into their fold, and similar attempts by Protestant Missions have ended in equal failure. The first attempt at regenerating their Church, and bringing them back from the barbarism to which years of isolation and neglect had reduced them, was made at the time when

tradition of St. Thomas having preached the gospel in India, in the 47th Chapter of the "Decline and Fall."

Colonel Macaulay was British Resident. It was then that the pious, noble-hearted and energetic Buchanan strove to emancipate the fallen Syrians from that degradation and obscurity in which they had been so long immersed.

These schismatics, who chiefly lived in a place "five days' march through the woods, which no European had yet visited," are the poor Syrians; and their locality, described as "remote and situated in impenetrable forests where jungle fever and tigers abound," and before going to which Buchanan felt it prudent "to put his house in order," in the pleasant Missionary station of Cottayam, one of the most charming spots in all Travancore. Here it was that Buchanan laid the basis of that intercourse with the Syrians that eventually resulted in their rescue from the blind state of ignorance into which they had fallen. That the praiseworthy efforts to bring them over to the Protestant Church have in a measure failed, is not from any deficiency or lack of zeal or perseverance on the part of those who worked in so worthy a cause. All honour to those who strove so manfully for the sake of their fellow-creatures. It is more than consolation to know that however short the aim may have fallen of its ultimate object, a vast deal of intelligence, education and moral good has been diffused among a stray flock, who previously were wandering without a shepherd and sunk in indolence and sloth.

It was previous to Buchanan's visit that La Croze, a French Protestant, attempted to make inquiries into the state of the Syrian Churches in Travancore, and the result of his investigations will be found in his "Histoire du Christianisme des Indes," published at La Hague in 1724. An admirable account of this long lost branch of the Church of Antioch may be found in a small publication entitled the "Syrian Church of India," written by Dr. Macbride, and printed at Oxford in 1856.

I have remarked above on the lovely situation of Cottayam, where the Church of England has long established a mission. Writing of the place, Mr. Tucker says, "the mountains in the distance, and the open space of hill and dale immediately before us, and the Cottayam river winding round, leave an impression on my mind of peaceful beauty and fertility and repose, which years of turmoil and occupation have been unable to efface. Below, by the river's side, is the old college, built under the direction of Colonel Munro, picturesque but inconvenient. On the higher ground stands the new college built by the Society, with its chapel, library, lecture-rooms and apartments, forming three sides of a quadrangle. Behind, and where the river passes out of sight among the trees, stands out the upper Syrian Church with its elevated chancel, and lower down the second Syrian and Roman Catholic Churches."

It was fortunate that such men as Macaulay and Munro were in those days the British Residents in Travancore, for the Rajah was much inclined to promote the welfare of his Christian subjects, and these British plenipotentiaries brought their powerful influence to bear upon the good cause. Arrangements were made, with the sanction of the reigning prince, for erecting a college at Cottayam for the educational training of the Syrian youth, and with the view of aiding also in the religious and moral education of the priests.

I remained four days at Cochin, and then again embarked on board the *Antelope*, a Residency boat, for Quilon. I had now a voyage of four-and-twenty hours before me without any stoppages, and consequently with regard to the future had laid in a stock of provisions for that time. The scenery of the backwater is very monotonous, and yet possesses a charm of its own. The masses of cocoa-palms which line the banks on both sides are, from their peculiar foliage and natural gracefulness, singularly picturesque. Occasionally the waters opened out into a wider space, and then again contracted. At times we passed by small islands, and now and then had to pass through some narrow canals, yet still around and everywhere were the everlasting cocoa-palms. About six in the evening we entered the Bay of Allepey—the most extensive sheet of water in the whole part of this sea-inlet. It measures about ten miles in width and twenty in length, so that one shore cannot be seen from the opposite. In rough weather the waves rise here to a considerable height, and the boatmen invariably under a suspicious sky hug the shore and keep close inland.

Having now entered the country I must say a few words about the charming and attractive province of Travancore, which is situated in the south-western corner of the Indian Peninsula, at the base of the lower extremities of the Western Ghauts. Although a tributary state of the British Government under the Madras Presidency, yet its comparative smallness and isolation has contributed more or less to keep it outside the range of much observation until the last twenty or thirty years, when many causes, and notably education, together with the liberal and praiseworthy spirit of its Rajahs and their ministers, has prominently brought the principality into notice, insomuch that it has recently earned, and deservedly so, the title of the "Model State."

Regarding its early history it will be sufficient to allude here to its connection with the English powers, which dates back from about the beginning of this century, or a little earlier. When Tippoo was devastating the fairest provinces of Southern India, and endeavouring to compel to forcible conversion to Islamism those Hindoo communities whose towns were sacked and destroyed by his licentious soldiery, events brought them by degrees to the hitherto peaceful and remote territories belonging to the Rajah of Travancore. The armies soon hovered over the borders of this and the neighbouring State of Cochin, and the Rajah, naturally alarmed for his throne and his country, invited the aid of the British Government at the Presidency in arresting the march of the cruel hordes of Tippoo's freebooters. In return for their services, thus opportunely rendered, a protective treaty was made with the British authorities, placing Travancore as a tributary state under the paramount power of the East India Company. Several local disturbances took place at various intervals, before the country was thoroughly tranquillized. These arose from factious opposition stirred up the Dewans and other parties hostile to foreign invasion; but they were ultimately quelled, and peace and prosperity under the ægis of British rule was guaranteed to the country, and an era of progress and civilization has since gradually commenced, which promises, as years go on, to bear much good and deserved fruit.

Its natural scenery is of that singularly fresh and verdant character peculiar to the other parts of the western coast. The heavy periodical rains, prevailing with but slight intermission for nine months in the year, give birth to a profuse vegetation. The magnificent line of ghauts on its eastern boundary is most grand and attractive, at times rising abruptly in bare and rocky peaks, and now covered from the foot to the summit with dense and pathless forests, and overhanging the low plains from the heights of from 5,000 to 6,000 feet above the sea level. The main chain runs for about 150 miles to Cape Comorin, with occasional deep depressions, and terminates in a bold precipitous mass, some 3,000 feet high, within twelve miles of the Cape itself. The mountains are loftiest at the extreme north of the country, where they stretch east and west for sixty or seventy miles, separating the districts of Dindigul and Madura, and rising into peaks of from 6,000 to 7,000 feet, which overhang the plains of Coimbatore. They are generally very precipitous, and undulating grassy ridges seem to be of common occurrence at very high elevations. My friend, the late Mr. Broun, who was the director for many years of His Highness's Observatory at Trevandrum, and whose scientific attainments earned for him the just praise of the savans of Europe, in writing of the approach to one of his meteorological stations on these mountains, says, "The huge wall of the Western Ghauts was always before us, appearing to rise higher and higher the nearer we approached the base; and around us were the haunts of the elephant, the tiger, the leopard, and the wild boar. * * Before us, at Attray Mallay, a wall descends vertically upwards of 500 feet, the clefts and ledges dotted with the mountain-palm: the steep sloping base is hidden by forests of the bastard bamboo, and on one side the slopes of the range are covered with forests almost as varied in colour as in early autumn in England. * * On gaining the summit we saw Travancore lying to the west below us, spotted with shade and bright sunshine. The next morning we began the ascent of the Agustia peak, descending about 1,000 feet: the route, an elephant track, was a stream of water running over large rolled masses of granite, till we attained the northern spur called Podia Mallay. Here we had glimpses to the east of the burning red plains of Tinnevelly." Such is a truthful description of the wild mountainous scenery, now perhaps seldom, if ever, traversed. On the coast again the shores are belted with the cocoa, areca, and other palms, in the midst of which lie embosomed the villages or separate huts and gardens of the natives, giving an air of calmness and gentle repose to the beautiful landscape.

But a peculiar feature of this country lies in the existence of an extensive backwater, which stretches at the present time without intermission from the capital itself to Chowghaut, in the British territory, in all about 175 miles. It is only very recently that the last barrier of intervening land has been pierced, and that between Trevandrum and Quilon. Canals in other places have at various intervals been dug in order to form a continuous line of water-way through the entire route. The depths as well as the widths are various throughout; the latter, as in the case of the Bay of Allepey, having a stretch from shore to shore of about ten miles across, forming quite a miniature inland sea. The utility of this water communication throughout the entire length of the country it may be easy to imagine, and it certainly must prove to be of most essential benefit to both trade and transit. The low lands on the shores of or beyond this backwater, and actually cultivable, vary in width from twelve to thirty miles, gradually opening from the neighbourhood of Cape Comorin to those wider parts adjoining the territories of the Cochin Rajah in the north.

The principal inhabitants of the country are called Nairs, or Warriors, and constitute the third division of the Sudra caste of Brahmins. In complexion they are remarkably fair, and the almost European colour of their skin, in contrast with their jet-black hair, gives to the women a very handsome appearance. Whatever may have been said or believed of their bravery and courage as a warrior race in earlier days, can hardly apply to their descendants in the present day. They are singularly docile and gentle, and the appellation once given to them of "born soldiers," must be received reservedly. In "Johnson's Relations of the Famous Kingdoms of the World," a quaint volume of travels published in 1611, it is written of these Nairs—"They inhabit no towns, but dwell in houses made of earth environed with hedges and woods, and their ways as intricate as into a labyrinth. It is strange to see how ready the soldier of this country is at his weapons; they are all gentlemen and termed Nairs. At seven years of age they are put to school to learn the use of their weapons, where, to make them nimble and active, their sinews and joints are stretched by skilful fellows, and anointed with the oil Sesamus: by this anointing they become so light and nimble that they will wind and turn their bodies as if they had no bones, casting them backward, forward, high and low, even to the astonishment of the beholders. Their continual delight is in their weapons, persuading themselves that no nation goeth beyond them in skill and dexterity." Such was a picture of the Nairs in former days. The skilful management of their weapons must I fear be now reckoned among one of the lost arts.

It would perhaps surprise an Englishman suddenly landing on the coast of Travancore, and whose imagination may previously have imbibed notions of the dusky races of Hindostan, to come in contact with the elegant forms and fair complexions of the high-caste Nairs. I have always found them to be most courteous and affable in their bearing, and in regard to their social qualities fit to hold their own against any Europeans.

Of course they have customs peculiar to themselves. Among others, it is considered a mark of gentility to carry an umbrella. These are made of the dried leaves of the Palmyra or Cocoa-palm and furnished with a long bamboo handle. They are very broad at the top, slightly rounded, and notwithstanding their size are very light, and admirably adapted for keeping off either the rain or sun's rays. The natives, however, do not specially use them for such purposes. Day or night, rain or shine, the "Chattree" is indispensable, much as an Englishman would use his walking-stick, and I remarked that my servants on coming into Travancore immediately provided themselves with one so as not to be behind the world.

Among the Travancoreans generally the customs of deciding points in law are singular enough. In doubtful cases, where no proof can be obtained, the parties must be bound by the most solemn oaths, and where a dispute arises between creditor and debtor they both go together to the Pagoda, and each giving a coin the value of a shilling to the priest, they are taken to a wooden post, upon which the creditor lays a large sum of money equal to that to which he lays claim. This is equivalent to an attestation before their god of the lawfulness of the debt, which the other party is bound to pay.

It may readily be believed that this people are abandoned to many superstitious practices. To enumerate all would fill volumes. I can but glance at them here. The higher castes will never inhabit a newly-built house till it has been purified and consecrated by the priests, because the builders, who are a lower caste, must have defiled it. A great ceremony is gone through consequently before the owner occupies it. Among other doings an idol is carried three times round the building to the sound of a trumpet, and then deposited at the eastern door. They are very particular about the east door. When they go out for the first time in the morning it must always be through this entrance, which is considered lucky, because from it they first see the morning sun, before which they bend with reverence. In commencing the building of a house the first prop must be put up on the east side. The carpenters open three or four cocoa-nuts, spilling the juice as little as possible, and put some bits of Betel leaf into them, and from the way these latter float in the liquid they profess to calculate whether the house will be lucky or otherwise, whether it will stand for a long or short period, and so on. Of course they are believers in transmigration. It is considered a piece of great good fortune to transmigrate into the body of a white cow, but to pass into that of a buffalo is just the reverse, as that animal undergoes a great deal of rough treat-

F 2

ment, and is generally an object of aversion and contempt. They believe that during the intermediate period of a hundred years the souls of the departed often visit their descendants on earth. In order to give them a welcome they have a small hut prepared in which is a bench, and on this they place a cup of toddy, a kind of palm-wine. Sometimes they put some rice there saved from their meals, or strew grains on the ground for the refreshment of these spirits. The crows, who abound and are useful scavengers, derive the chief benefit from these scatterings. Witchcraft and the influence of the evil eye are also believed in to an incredible extent. They also have lucky and unlucky days. Monday and Thursday come under the latter category, and Sunday under the former. The last day of the month is very unlucky. It is a bad omen to meet a cat or a snake on first going out in the morning, and they will even turn back to avoid it; this they will also do if a crow flies past on the left hand. It is considered a good sign to sneeze with the face towards the house you are quitting, but unlucky if with the face turned in the direction in which you are going.

Trials by ordeal were frequently resorted to in this country. If a man was charged with any serious crime which he refused to confess, a pan containing cocoa-nut oil was brought and heated in the presence of Brahmins. The accused was then called upon to make a confession, and in the event of refusal, he was required to plunge his thumb and two first fingers in the boiling oil and pull out a ring placed at the bottom of the pan. A doctor then came and bound up the fingers with betel leaves, which were left on for three days; if at the end of this time the flesh where the skin had been burnt off was white, he was pronounced innocent, if black, he was punished as a perjured man.

Another ordeal was by snakes, especially cobras. In case of denial of a crime, one of these reptiles was wrapped up in a cloth, and the accused was required to thrust his hand in and seize the poisonous animal. If bitten, he was considered guilty. Another ordeal took place in a river or tank where alligators are found. The "Alligators' Pagoda," on the Cranganoor river close to Paliport, in the Cochin territory, was in former times especially famous for this process. A small pagoda, or heathen temple, stands on the bank of the river, in which two alligators were especially supported, their daily food having been thrown into the water in order to keep them there. To undergo this ordeal the accused was compelled to swim across this river and back, which if he refused to do, he was dragged through, holding on with his hands to a boat. If the alligator pulled him under the water, it was considered a sign of guilt, if otherwise, he was released as innocent.

Of course these trials by ordeal belong to a past age, and are no longer resorted to. But they are curious as records of customs now passed away from countries where more civilized institutions have taken their place. They consider the cobra a most sacred reptile. They actually reverence this creature, and keep a bit of their gardens partitioned off in honour of them for the chance of their coming. I had a ruined outhouse which I wanted to pull down, but my servants begged me not. I found that a cobra had taken up its abode there, and they used to feed it daily. They would sooner desert a building than eject a cobra if once it occupies a dwelling. I knew a case where an Arab merchant, who was on the point of sailing with a cargo of cocoanuts from the port of Cochin, discovered a large cobra in the hold of the vessel. He gave strict orders that it should be fed and carefully preserved, as the safety of the vessel would depend upon the animal's life. Whenever the natives find a dead cobra they burn its body with a piece of sandalwood, a grain of gold, coral, and other things, using the same ceremonies as they would at the funeral of a man of high caste. European soldiers and sailors sometimes turn this custom to good account. They kill a cobra and sell it to the natives, who eagerly buy it for the sake of giving it a good funeral.

The lower as well as the upper classes are divided into castes differing in rank and dignity. It will suffice to allude but to one or two. The Chegos are principally occupied in drawing toddy, which is compulsory on their caste. The

Pulleahs are a very low caste, and compose the greater portion of the slave population; but low as they are they will never admit their inferiority to a still lower class called the Caanekars. In every deep there is a lower deep. The latter maintain that their caste ranks highest, whilst the Pulleahs aver that they enjoy more privileges, and one is that they may employ barbers, and may wear a fillet on their heads and a long garment reaching to their knees which a Caanekar may not do. They are all miserable creatures. They are never allowed to come near the town, and even in the villages, I have seen them when they wish to purchase rice first deposit their piece of money about twenty paces in front of the shop, and then retire to a certain distance. The shopkeeper then comes out, takes up the money and places the rice down, and after he has gone in again the poor slave advances and takes up his purchase. Twenty yards is the nearest distance which a low caste person may approach a higher cast—but when a Brahmin comes along the road you see the people scattering themselves right and left, on both sides, to make way for the purer being who must not be polluted by closer contact. Some castes live entirely in the jungles. Among these are the Ollares, who collect honey and wax in the forests, where those articles are found in great abundance. These people wear little or no clothing and regard the tiger as their uncle. When one of these animals dies, either naturally or by violence, the Ollares shave their heads in token of mourning, and eat no cooked food for three days: they may eat no flesh but that of animals which have been killed by tigers, so the existence of these wild beasts is of some consideration to them. The Naiaddys are another low jungle race. They subsist almost entirely upon the flesh of the wild beasts they kill in hunting, as well as upon roots and herbs. Rice or any such luxurious food is unknown to them. They build a kind of dwelling in trees in order to avoid the attacks of wild animals. They have little or no clothing, and I should say, without exception, they form the most wretched outcast race on the face of the earth. They are very stunted in growth. I have found them very useful in tracking wild animals. In fact for this work they are invaluable, and degraded as they are, they yet have their uses.

The Brahmins are, of course, the highest caste in this country. Even the Royal Family rank second to them. Their religious influence is considerable, for their priestly character invests them with a sanctity reverenced by every other class in the country. The increasing intercourse with the outer world effects a silent but no less certain alteration of feeling and belief towards the sacred caste by the inferior classes, and the Brahmins have a feeling among themselves that in the course of fifty years their rule will have passed away. But at present the power and authority they exert either for good or evil is very great among their countrymen, and a number of years must elapse before the awe they inspire quite dies away. When I was at Cape Comorin the Brahmins had represented to the Rajah that in consequence of the scarcity of rain the crops would certainly fail; but that they were prepared to offer up prayers in the Pagoda for rain, but then it would be incumbent on him to send 1,700 fanams (equal to about £25) as an offering to the god! The money came while I was there. But where was the rain? Echo answered—where? It is a law that no Brahmin dies of starvation in Travancore. Such an event could not happen. The fact of his being a Brahmin invests him with a sanctity sufficient to shield him from all temporal wants. Thousands upon thousands of these classes are daily fed throughout the country gratuitously by the State. Houses are built for their especial reception and entertainment, and to want is a word unknown in their vocabulary. On certain festivals the Rajah distributes a certain amount of money to every Brahmin, man, woman, and child, who present themselves before him at a specified place and hour, and on such occasions parents bring every disposable child in order to receive the greater amount. It was seldom made a subject of strict inquiry whether the children were the *bonâ fide* offspring of those who brought them. In all probability they seldom were. However it so happened that even infants in arms were liable to no scrutiny whatever, and a woman who came with a child wrapt in swaddling clothes received the same bounty for her little one as for herself. One day one of the Rajah's almoners, more zealous or conscientious than his fellows, took it into his head to interrogate one of the women standing before him as a recipient of the king's bounty, and said, "Are you sure it *is* a child and not a lump of clothes you have got on your arm?" "Of *course* it is a child," replied the indignant mamma; "take care, take care—the poor thing, it is very sick—there, don't uncover it for the world, it will be killed by the cold air." But the suspicion of the official was roused, and he resolved to make a further examination. He pulled the clothes off rather violently, and true enough there was a child—but it was *dead!* It appeared that this deception had been carried on for a long time, and in all probability, after the excitement caused by this shocking revelation had subsided, the same practices occurred again. I will here relate another story illustrative of the habits of these people, showing one way by which they endeavour to obtain justice. A few evenings ago a woman, about thirty-five years of age, who had had a lawsuit pending for about ten or twelve years, lost all patience at the dilatory proceedings of the law. It appears that at last the suit had been decided in her favour, and a sum of money to which she became entitled was ordered to be paid her. But the Court's decree was one thing and payment another, and she seemed as far off as ever from handling her rightful coin. So she went and scaled a large tree in front of the Rajah's palace in a very populous part of the fort. Taking a large clasp-knife with her, she cried out at the top of her voice on purpose to attract a crowd, and if possible the Rajah's attention, and then she declared that if the money she was entitled to were not brought within an hour and deposited at the foot of the tree where she then was, she would plunge the knife in her breast, and her blood would then be upon the Rajah and his government officers. The crowd begged her to come down and abstain from doing anything so rash, and one official declared on the Rajah's authority that payment was guaranteed to her the moment she came down. "I shall *not* come down," she cried. "My death I know, and *you* know also, will bring eternal disgrace on the Rajah and his government, and I will never descend from this tree alive unless I see the bag of money deposited at the bottom of the tree—and that too speedily." The threats of this determined woman had the desired effect. The money was brought and placed at the foot of the tree, and she came down and walked off triumphantly. I was assured by a native that such scenes are by no means of unfrequent occurrence, and that she would not have hesitated to have carried out her threats if the money had not been forthcoming. Being fatalists, they have but little concern either for shedding their own or the blood of others. They will enter a person's house and rob it where no resistance is offered, but they will often murder the owner for mere wantonness and not from any feeling of revenge. The gallows has no terrors for them.

I now return from this digression upon the customs and habits of the people to a continuation of my journey, or, I should say, voyage, down the backwater. Allepey is connected with the latter by an artificial canal about three miles in length. There is nothing whatever attractive in the town, which is a busy, bustling, dirty place of trade; but there is a very singular thing connected with the roadstead which must not pass unnoticed, and this is the formation of an immense bank of mud in the open sea of about three miles in length, and of a considerable breadth, which has the effect of a natural breakwater, and which forms on it or inside it a perfectly secure anchorage for vessels even in the stormiest weather. This has given to Allepey the name of "Mud Bay." It is difficult to account for this formation. There is no doubt that the mud comes from the fresh waters of the lakes and is thrown up again by the action of the sea—but then there is no outlet or river within many miles of Allepey, and this has led to the supposition of there being a subterranean communication through which the deposit is carried. The bank is by no means stationary. It has been calculated to have shifted two or three miles in the last fifty years. A similar mud bank exists at Narrakul, a village on the coast, about three miles north of Cochin, and the immense advantage of this latter place as a natural open harbourage for shipping during the monsoons has been acknowledged by the Government. The mud imparts a dirty colour to the water and makes it very thick and slimy.

On emerging from the Allepey Canal there is a very deep bay, a favourite resort of alligators, which at mid-day may be seen basking on the banks with their huge mouths wide open. They seemed to be accustomed to the noise of the oars and we passed close by them,—but I occasionally roused them from their noonday siesta by a rattling bullet from my rifle, which, if it failed to kill them, sent them splashing into the water in an instant. I one time made a successful shot by lodging a bullet in the brain of one about seven feet long. He scarcely gave a struggle—but just turned over on his side and died in an instant. Their skin is so tough that a ball glances off unless it penetrates some softer part and enters either the brain or heart. I have never heard that the skin is made any use of, but alligators' eggs are readily sought after by the natives, and are sold in the bazaars as articles of food among the poorer classes.

As soon as we had crossed the bay we entered some very narrow canals, and in some places the water was so shallow that the men had to get out and haul the boat over the mud. Over one of these canals we came to a very singular bridge, very simple in structure, but quaint in appearance, and on the other side of this bridge was a remarkable object in the water, which, on nearer approach, I observed to be a life-size figure of a man cut out in stone. It was half-way out of the water, slightly bending over, with the arms stretched out. As we passed it I overheard the boatmen muttering something and making signs among themselves, upon which I concluded it must be some idol or river-god, under whose especial care the bridge might originally have been placed. But no such thing. The legend tells that it is the body of a murderer, who, after he had slain his victim, a woman, ran for his escape into the water for the purpose of reaching the opposite shore, but that an avenging Providence overtook him ere he had gone many paces, and he was turned into stone while in the act of running away, and has remained in that position ever since. The signs made by my boatmen and the prayers they uttered are invariably resorted to whenever they pass the stone murderer. The appearance is very peculiar but grotesque. It is exactly the position of a man in the act of running with his arms upraised as if about to plunge into deeper water, and it would be curious to ascertain on what account it was really made and placed there.

I arrived at Quilon about 9 A.M., and was very glad to get again on shore after the long confinement of the boat. I now prepared to pass through a belt of forest of about sixty-five miles to Courtallum, on the other side of the mountains. Leaving the Residency about mid-night, I set off in a palanquin, intending to get over about twenty-five miles before morning, but the roads were so bad and my bearers so intoxicated that I found at daybreak that I had still eight more miles to get over. Seeing how hopeless it was going on in the palanquin, I got out and walked the remaining distance through the solitary jungle; yet in spite of much shade from the large trees I found the heat very distressing, and did not arrive at my rendezvous till 9.30. This place is completely hemmed in by dense forests, though two or three villages manage to find room enough to exist therein, and enable the traveller to obtain some scanty supplies. Few ever travel this road, and even they only at certain seasons when there is no fever. Of course wild animals are very abundant, especially elephants, which at times are very troublesome. Extensive plantations of coffee run on both sides of the road a great part of the way, where the jungle has been cleared for the purpose. Besides coffee, there are plantations of nutmegs, sugar, cinnamon, and even tea, though the latter is only experimental.

Courtallum, where I arrived in due course, is the Spa of Southern India, situate at the foot of the Eastern Ghauts in the Tinnevelly country. It is resorted to as a sanitarium by Europeans during the prevalence of the south-west monsoon. For its three or four months of season the air is cool and temperate, and consequently the place affords a very pleasant retreat from the hot winds and scorched plains of the Carnatic during the most unpleasant of seasons on the latter coast. The cool, refreshing waters of a mountain stream, forming in its course three or four fine waterfalls, afford one of the most striking features of the surrounding scenery, and according to the prevalence of rain on the Western Ghauts the cascades are more or less violent and grand. A large pool at the foot of the largest is secured for bathing, where accommodation for all parties is made available. The wind at times is very violent as it rushes through the passes, but as it comes with refreshing showers, it is always acceptable, and it is this which renders the locality so attractive and desirable. The frequent showers which pass along the sides of the hills do not extend their influence beyond the distance of a couple of miles, so that standing at the Residency and looking towards the west I see nothing but clouds and rain, and towards the east nothing but clear sky and sunshine. Of course those limits, so much influenced by the rain, are garbed in constant verdure, so refreshing to the eye, for the passing showers

> Are an eternal April to the ground,
> Making it all one emerald.

And I may add, an eternal March also, for the name of "Hurricane Hall," given to one of the chief houses, testifies to the boisterous nature of the climate.

While in this neighbourhood I enjoyed a great deal of sport, as game of all kinds was abundant, both at the foot and on the summit of these mountains. But the sport that far exceeds all others is that of elephant shooting, of which I had a little experience in these forests. I hear many people declaiming against this kind of shooting on account of the sagacity and usefulness of that noble animal; but these philotherists (if I may coin such an expression) do not or care not to consider the other side of the picture. "What with elephants at night and wild hogs in the morning," was the pitiable expression of a poor ryot to me once, "it is hard for a poor man to live on his cultivation." They who have seen the utter desolation done to the crops in one night by a single elephant, much more a whole herd, must admit that the destruction ot a few of these brutes occasionally is more desirable than otherwise.

It must have been Alexander the Great who

first indulged in an elephant hunt. He appears to have enjoyed a little sport on his own account on the banks of the Indus, perhaps in those identical jungles which formed the famous Shikargahs of the late Ameers of Scinde. On this subject Arrian, in his Expedition of Alexander, says: "There are, however, many Indians who are hunters of elephants, and whom Alexander was anxious to keep near him. With their assistance he gave chase after the elephants. Two, during a pursuit, fell down a precipice and perished. The rest were captured, and keepers being appointed for them, they were subsequently attached to the army." However, it must be remembered that after all these were tame animals which, after an action in which Alexander had been engaged, had been left behind by the flying enemy. The credit therefore of having hunted the elephant in its wild state must be given to Pompey the Great, for we read in his life by Plutarch that, while in Numidia, "He chose not to leave the savage beasts in the desert without giving them a specimen of Roman valour and success. Accordingly he spent a few days in hunting lions and elephants." There can be no mistake about their being wild ones, for we know that the African species, in contradistinction to the Asiatic, inhabits open plains and deserts, and not forests. The mode of capturing wild elephants as described in detail by Arrian is in almost all points similar to that practised at the present day in Ceylon; but Sir E. Tennent has so exhausted the subject in his book on the latter country that no further mention need be made here. I shall content myself with detailing my own experiences, though possibly a very unworthy follower of such mighty Nimrods as those alluded to.

The usual mode of entrapping wild elephants in the forests of Southern India is by digging deep pits, sometimes to the number of two hundred in one locality. The places selected are generally in a valley between two hills which may be the usual *run* of the animals, or else some solitary secluded spot near their accustomed haunts, not far from a river. These pits are lightly covered with a layer of thin bamboo or other sticks, and over this frame-work are scattered dead leaves, in order to make the surface as natural as possible, for the elephant is most wary and cunning; and I have seen where they have walked securely on the brinks between a row of pits, knowing as they must that one false step would have precipitated them into the deep hole prepared for them. The great objection to the pit system is the injury which the animal receives in its fall, as might be expected when such a weighty mass tumbles headlong a depth of twenty feet or more. In most cases the damage it receives quite incapacitates the beast for future use. Another difficulty, too, is how to take the animal out of the pit again. The first thing is to throw in a quantity of branches of trees, leaves and rubbish, so as to bring the animal to the highest elevation consistent with safety. His legs and neck must then be secured with chains. Two or three tame ones are kept in readiness, and the same chains are fastened to them, when all being firmly bound and a signal given, the captive is dragged out by sheer force. I recollect on one occasion that one—a powerful male—struggled so violently that he had scarcely been brought to the ground outside the pit's mouth than he dropped down dead, having burst a blood-vessel from the vehemence of his struggles to get free.

Our tents were once pitched in the heart of a forest so dense that we could hardly see further than forty or fifty yards in any direction. Early one morning intelligence was brought me that an elephant had been destroying a patch of dry cultivation during the night, scarcely a quarter of a mile from our encampment. I instantly set off, gun in hand, with two or three trackers in search of the destroyer. On coming to the ground there was unmistakable evidence of the marauder, for, judging by his huge footmarks, he must have been revelling and capering about in the dry grain all night. I now put myself into the hands of the guide, who promised to bring me up to the beast. After some beating about in the grain we at last traced him to the edge of a jungle, and now that we knew which road he had taken, it was only a matter of time when we should come up to him. So we began to follow his track, and it became evident from the freshness of the footprints that he could not be very far ahead, and would probably be found quietly feeding in some shady dell in our circuit. Such, at least, was the conjecture of my guide. We now trod the ground very softly, taking care not to make the slightest noise either by treading incautiously on dry leaves or broken sticks, for of the elephant the hearing is wonderfully acute, and he is off at the least unusual sound. We walked in file. First went the guide with my two ounce rifle. I followed with a large double-barrel gun, and behind me again was a native with a third fowling-piece. My heart beat as we threaded with slow and cautious steps the still and awful solitudes of the forest. We scarcely allowed ourselves to breathe, and the silence around us was solemn and unearthly. Every now and then the guide would stop and raise his hand as if hearing some distant noise—perhaps the elephant itself. This was an exciting moment. All ears were strained to catch the slightest murmur. But no—it was an illusion, and we proceeded on once more. It was now about an hour since we had entered the forest, and I began to think we might yet have a long chase, so I called a halt, and after resting about ten minutes we moved on again. We had scarcely gone a hundred yards when the guide suddenly stopped, raised his hand, when we all instinctively halted and listened. Hark! The crash of a bough not thirty yards off. It was the elephant. We had come up to him at last. Another crash! A third! He was feeding and tearing down the branches of a tree. On going a little further we found he was in the middle of such a dense jungle that we stood to deliberate how we should reach him, for I wanted to face him at about twelve or fifteen paces and fire into his head. There was no alternative but to enter the patch of jungle on hands and knees, creeping stealthily among the bamboos without being able to see three yards round us in any way. Another crash! We were fast closing on the brute. On we crept slowly, hoping to emerge in some open spot where we might get a fair and open view. But what if he were to hear or smell us beforehand, and rush towards us while we were on all-fours! Never mind. *Audaces fortuna juvat.* And our perseverance was at last crowned with success. We found a comparatively open spot, and peeping out we gazed upon a fine male elephant with a noble pair of tusks. He ceased eating and stared at us intruders. The foremost guide stepped back. I advanced a few paces, cocking my gun. The elephant charged at me. I raised my fowling-piece and fired at his head. He was not twenty paces from me. The blow stopped him and he staggered, pausing for an instant as if preparing to charge again. I turned round for a second gun wherewith to give him the "coup de grâce," when he rushed off, roaring and bellowing with a noise that made the forest echo again. And it was fortunate for me that the animal had found discretion the better part of valour, for when I turned round for my other guns I found myself *alone.* Every native had run away—the arrant cowards! If they had remained staunch and handed me a second gun I could scarcely have failed to have secured my game. But I was not disappointed after all. When the natives returned, on finding all was safe, we tracked the animal up, and the blood on his track showed that he was severely wounded.

The guides promised to return next day and look for him. They were true to their word—and the animal was found dead near a river bank not very far from where I first shot at him. I claimed the tusks as a trophy, and they were given to me by the authorities.

It is evident that little or no dependence can be placed upon a native when there exists any likelihood of danger in the pursuit of large game; but, after all, their conduct under such circumstances is scarcely blamable, considering they share in none of the excitement, while they must partake of all the risk. I certainly have known cases, but rarely, of a native keeping his presence of mind on these occasions. Even in a crisis they can far more easily slink under a bush than a dressed European, and so escape detection. In cases of great danger they have been known to throw off their turban or upper loose garment to attract the elephant's attention while they convey themselves away in safety to a distance. The enraged animal will satisfy his rage by tearing the cloak into a thousand shreds, and then pass on as if sufficiently revenged.

CHAPTER III.

Politicals in India — General Cullen—Journal—Cape Comorin — Travancore — Trevandrum — Durbar at Tanjore—Fights of Animals—An Elephant Ride.

AMONG the many divisions of authority peculiar to our Indian Empire there exists a class of high functionaries appointed to preside over the interests, for good or evil, of the protected states recognized by the British Government. These magnates are elected from the qualified members of the civil and military services, and are variously dubbed, according to circumstances, Commissioners, Political Agents, Envoys, Residents, and so on. And many able men there have been among them, and a vast amount of good have they accomplished in behalf of their own Government, as well as of that wherein they have chanced to reside. Their official duties resemble those of the Roman Proconsul of old, and if an occasional

Verres has crept in among them, it has been quite the exception; and the names of Lawrence, Pottinger, and Burnes will testify to the sterling worth of such administrators, in spite of Sir Charles Napier's sneer at the "boy politicals." In the Madras Presidency there were three men of remarkable ability, holding the highest appointments in this branch of the service, and all belonging to the army. They were known as the Triumvirate—men, perhaps, of lesser note than those mentioned above, only because they worked in a limited sphere and, perhaps, *Carent quia vate sacro.*

It was my good fortune to have been officially connected with one of the above politicals for upwards of twelve years. General Cullen was a man of rare merit, who, in despite of the shortcomings of his early education, contrived to attain the highest honours in the Presidency where he served. His capabilities were early recognized by Sir Frederick Adam when Governor of Madras, with whom he contracted a personal friendship and correspondence, only ending at the death of the latter. He was then Commissary-General, and when under Lord

Elphinstone's tenure of office the Residency of Travancore fell vacant, General Cullen was at once nominated to the vacant post. It is the only political appointment of the kind in the Madras Presidency, Mysore and Hyderabad being in the gift of the Governor-General. For twenty years he conducted the onerous and responsible duties of Resident; and although his good name was at times attacked by the agents of a scurrilous press, yet those who knew him intimately felt and acknowledged how undeserved were these libels, hatched and uttered by adventurous and discontented Europeans, whose only real grievances were those of jealousy and disappointed ambition. Among the missionaries it was in some respects a misfortune that, in reference to public acts, he was not always on the best of terms, not from any fault of his own, but he felt that his policy must be shaped first in the interests of the Prince whose dominions were under his supervision, and that he could not always, in consistency with his duties as adviser to the Rajah, yield in every point to the somewhat preposterous claims of the missions. Yet were the truth known and confessed as I know it, no one could have been more liberal in pecuniary gifts to the several missions whenever any reasonable request for support was made to him. A refined and courteous gentleman by birth and manners, he was especially fitted to win real friends in private life, and in society his fund of information and anecdote would have made him a welcome guest and companion, had he not been a sufferer from the distressing calamity of deafness, which precluded him from sharing the hospitality of others, or often according it himself. Hence his popularity outside his immediate circle of friends never increased, and his motives were misunderstood. I will not speak here of his scientific attainments because they partook of too desultory a character to have left any permanent result for good, or if they did, it was in a very limited degree. He took up science as an amateur rather than as a professional, and to him it was, with few exceptions, little more than the pleasure of a lifetime. He was never married. On his retirement from Travancore the natives felt they had lost a friend and benefactor whom it would be difficult to replace.

At the present day the Government is carried on under the immediate management of the Dewan or Prime Minister, with his several subordinates and dependent officers of all grades and duties, His Highness of course being supreme in all important matters requiring his sanction and approval. The British Resident at the Court is accredited by the Madras Government as adviser to H.H. with almost unlimited authority as to the general supervision of affairs throughout the country. Under the provisions of the treaty the Travancore Government engaged to pay a subsidy of eight lacs of rupees annually, the British Government agreeing to protect the principality from foreign aggression and, furthermore, maintain a force of three native regiments of infantry, as well as artillery, at the station of Quilon. This number of troops has, however, been considerably reduced, and for many years past only one corps of infantry has been posted there. Whether this change in the original agreement has always been palatable to the Travancorians is no question to discuss here; yet I know that at one time, when the financial affairs of the State were not by any means flourishing, it was considered but fair that a proportionate reduction of the subsidy should have been made in consequence of the withdrawal of the troops. In addition to the Quilon regiment His Highness has a body of soldiers, consisting of two regiments about 600 strong each, composed entirely of Nairs, and this is known as the Nair Brigade, whose headquarters are at Trevandrum. They act as a kind of local militia, providing for the Pagoda Guards, police stations and jails throughout the country, and, further are required to assist in all the religious ceremonies and festival displays about the Court. The brigade is commanded by English officers selected from regiments in the Madras Presidency.

After a residence of some weeks at Courtallum we set out again on our journey to Travancore, and I record here a list of the Resident's marching establishment, which might astonish the good people at home, as it did myself on first acquaintance. Private servants 21, peons 13, palanquin bearers 13, torch bearers 2, lascars 7, washermen 2, apothecary and assistant, shoemaker, shepherd and flock of sheep, butcher and baker, carpenter, wine cooler. Coolies 200, carts 12, elephants 5, horses 6, dogs 6, bullocks 30, and besides these geese, turkeys, ducks, cows with their usual attendants. This is a pretty fair list, but in cases admitting of doubt, I have written down the number below the actual quantity. Besides these it must be recollected that most of these people have their families with them. Consider then what an encampment it is, especially as it includes a guard of 22 Sepoys, and their families also. And all these to serve for the luxury and comfort of one individual. We travelled now by short stages, varying from ten to twelve miles each. At Ayenkoil our tents were pitched in a thick grove about midway up a mountain pass. The locality was so shaded by lofty trees and dense foliage that we left the tent and dined *sub Jove.* The Resident came here purposely to examine some limestone caves. In the midst of the grove is a very ancient temple in ruins, so old that pieces of the roof and stone sides are clinging in mid air to branches of trees, which having been disconnected from the building have been hoisted up in this singular position. A stream of the clearest water runs through the middle of the building. One might fancy this spot was made for a Druid, or the goddess Ferona. While strolling about in the evening not far from this, I shot five flying foxes and gave them to the horsekeepers and other menials, who consider their flesh very good. My own servant, who would despise such rank fare, took my gun and shot himself a jay, which he pronounced "very fine eating," so forthwith walked off to make a curry of it. I envied neither the one nor the other their meals, however savoury.

I now kept a journal of our daily proceedings, from which I propose to make occasional extracts. Rode ten miles to Cape Comorin, and Horace could not have exulted more on reaching Brundusium than I did at arriving at this wild but charming spot. From the hot scorching plains to come in a morning's ride before breakfast to a fine large house on the sea-coast was inexpressibly delightful. We are surrounded on three sides by the ocean, and can see the sun rise and set beyond the waves.

There is a small village close by, with a pagoda, the former is called Kunnea Cumuru, from which is derived the modern name of Cape Comorin. A more retired spot in all India could scarcely be selected than this for those who are fond of a quiet life. I will not say a solitary one—for the sea, the restless, ever-changing sea is a companion one never tires of.

The beach was covered with fossil limestone, and in one part there in red garnet sand, and in another "Rice sand." This latter consists of smooth pieces of broken quartz the size of grains of rice, which by the action of the waves have become so rounded and polished that they appear exactly as if so much rice had been spilt; and the following legend accounts for it: What we call Cape Comorin the natives call *Kunnea Komari*, meaning the "Maiden Comaree," and the story runs that a beautiful young lady rejoicing in that name was the destined bride of a rich and handsome Prince. All things were made ready for the wedding. Heaps of rice and fruits, and all the concomitant delicacies of so auspicious an occasion were prepared, but the false bridegroom tarried and came not.

At last Comaree, impatient and sorrowful, took the bowls of rice, and in her vexation scattered them on the ground with a curse, hoping her faithless lover might eat the sand of the shore after the cruel disappointment she had experienced, and there is the "rice sand" in support of this pretty legend!

There is but scanty vegetation in the neighbourhood. Here and there are a few stunted cotton plants trying to exist in the sandy plains. The Palmyra palm is the only tree at all abundant. Nothing else could grow in such a wilderness. In fact the whole landscape is dreary enough, though the sense of utter isolation is broken by the background, where is seen the bold outline of the mountains reaching a height of some 5,000 feet, the extremity of that line of ghauts, which stretch down the entire length of the Western coast, and end in a black precipitous rock about fifteen miles from the Cape. We had little inducement to stay here long. Curiosity more than aught else had brought us so far. So we set off again. I was well mounted, and preferred this mode of marching to any other, as it enabled me to see the country through which I was passing. and which was all so new to me. There is a native legend accounting for the formation of the extensive coast line from Goa to Cape Comorin. In bygone ages the sea washed the foot of the mountain range which now lies several miles inland. The inhabitants who dwelt at the foot of these hills were all fishermen. It happened that there dwelt at a place called Gokurna near Goa a prophet renowned for his sanctity called Paroes Raman. Now his aged mother was a wicked woman, and to the great shame and sorrow of her son had acquired a name notorious for her evil deeds. In a fit of anger caused by such disgrace, the prophet seized a rice winnow, and hurled it with tremendous force from Gokurna right over the sea. By a miracle it was carried away as far as Cape Comorin; upon which all the sea between the two places immediately dried up and became that level tract of land known as Malabar. The prophet resolved to take up his abode in this new territory, together with his mother, where he hoped to hide her disgrace. In the meantime the fishermen whose daily occupations must have suffered a slight interruption from this sudden change of affairs, flocked to the lowlands to seek for the sea-coast. The prophet met them, and had no difficulty in persuading them to occupy the new territory, and with the view of their permanently settling there he invested them with the dignity of Brahmins, promising, as had always been his custom, to provide daily food for the 3,000 of their caste. He then took their fishing-nets, tore them into strands, which he twisted together to make three cords, which the Brahmins wear as a mark of their caste tied in a knot on the shoulder, and falling down below the waist. These Brahmins of Malabar are called Namboories, and are reproached by the other Brahmins for their descent from fishermen.

18th.—Rode to Oodeagherry. This is a fortified place now dismantled. It was built by a Frenchman some seventy or eighty years ago, named Launoy. His tomb is in the churchyard among several others.* Fra Bartolomeo in his

* His tombstone bears the following inscription :—Hic jacet Eustathius Benedictus de Launoy qui tanquam dux generalis militiæ Travancotidis præfuit ac per annos xxxvii

travels in this country says, writing about 1780, "I formed an acquaintance with M. Launoy at Casiapulli." It seems that he was a military adventurer in the Rajah of Travancore's service, to whom he rendered most effectual aid against the incursions of his hostile neighbour, the Rajah of Cochin. Inside this fortress are the remains of what was once a church, but of which only the bare walls remain. Church and tombs and graves are covered with almost impenetrable jungle, the retreat of leopards, one of which I caught alive in a trap and sent subsequently to the Rajah's menagerie in the town of Trevandrum.

19th.—Rode five miles to the foot of the hills near this place, and breakfasted in tents prepared for our reception. Then commenced the ascent, a distance of four miles. It was very steep and stony. On the summit were erected two temporary bungalows, which were fairly habitable in spite of the rains and mists which

fermè summà felicitate regi inserviit, cui omnia regna ex Caiamcolum usque ad Cochin vi armorum ac terrore subjecit. Vixit annos lxii menses V et mortuus die I Junii MDCCLXXVII. Requiescat in pace.—His son was killed in an excursion into Madura.

were prevailing. The elevation is about 2,000 feet above the sea—and the Resident has succeeded in raising potatoes and other vegetables. In one of the gardens I picked a few strawberries, which seem to thrive very well. The view embraces a very wide stretch of sea in the distance, and an endless succession of hill and valley. We remained here about three days. While sitting outside our tents one evening, some natives approached us, and from their manners and appearance we soon saw they were petitioners, and the following scene which took place will give an idea of the administration of British justice in gentle but summary fashion:—

About five or six natives advanced in a row, and commenced the drama by throwing themselves flat on their faces on the ground and commencing to howl. After this preliminary skirmishing they rose, and one of them advancing in a most timid but respectful manner, his petition written on the leaf of a palmyra, and held out at arm's length, as being the most respectful position he could assume, stood waiting to be called up. An interpreter is now summoned, and upon the coming of this actor on the scene the howling and bellowing increases tenfold, each trying to have his own case heard first. As a mere spectator I was vastly amused at what followed. The first "party" allowed to approach was an elderly-looking man with his wife and child, when the following scene took place:

Resident: What does that man want?

Interpreter: He complains, sir, that he had a very nice garden, but that it has been forcibly taken from him.

Res.: How long since has he been dispossessed?

Interp.: About a year ago. His complaint was disposed of some months ago, and the garden restored to him, but he has had it taken from him again.

Res.: Take his petition; it shall be inquired into. Who is that boy crying there? What does he want?

Interp.: He says, sir, his brother was murdered about eight years ago, and he demands satisfaction.

Res.: Good! We'll dispose of this hereafter.

In the meantime find out all about it, and let me know. Who's the next?

Interp.: That man with the hump-back, sir, declares that some enemy killed a cow and put the carcase into his house, and the owner of it comes and swears that he killed it, and demands compensation for its loss.

Res.: He's a very black-looking fellow. Where does he come from?

Interp.: Mentions a village a long way off.

Res.: Well, I think he had better take his complaint to his own country and have it settled there. No more cases? Take all the petitions, and we'll inquire into them by and by. Now tell them to be off.

Then commenced such a howling and crying. It was impossible to say which was loudest in his vociferations. The boy whose brother had been murdered didn't appear half satisfied at so summary a disposal of his case, and the man who had lost his garden seemed to give up all hopes of ever getting it back again. The cow-conspiracy man was the only one among the lot who went away contented, and certainly it was but fair that he should be judged, at least by his accusers, in their own country.

24th.—Arrived at Trevandrum about 6 P.M. A gig and horse were ready waiting for us at the Kurramunnay bridge, about a mile and a half from the Residency, and preceded by two torch-bearers, we drove through the town, and arrived in time for a welcome dinner. After this I was shown to my own future abode, apart from the Residency, on the opposite side of the high road. It was a most comfortable dwelling-house, lying in the midst of a fine spacious garden.

The day after my arrival at the capital, I went to pay a visit to His Highness the Rajah. The reigning Prince is accomplished and well-educated. His manners are frank and genial, and he is a living proof of the excellent system of English education which has been introduced into his country, not only for the benefit of himself and family, but especially for all his subjects.

His Highness received me in his palace. For a short time I was kept waiting, according to Eastern etiquette, in the anteroom, and while here I engaged in conversation with the Dewan or Prime Minister of State. I took the opportunity of examing the motley collection of furniture and decorations of the royal apartments. The fittings were more gaudy than neat, and there was an evident display more of outward show than of taste or refinement. Large mirrors, ottomans, statuary, clocks, couches, worked chairs, and all the concomitant et-ceteras of glitter and parade. These princes spare no money when tempted to gratify their curiosity by anything novel or attractive, and a good story is told of one of these scions of royalty, who, poring over the advertisements in the papers, as they constantly do, saw among other novelties, some "Fine Perukes" for sale. It puzzled His Highness to think what these were, whether they might be watches, or sweetmeats, or steam engines, or what not. It would have been *infra dig.* to have betrayed his ignorance by making any previous inquiry upon the subject, so he forthwith desired his favourite secretary to write and order a dozen of the finest perukes. The order was received; the perukes dispatched; one dozen of the finest perukes for

His Highness the Rajah of T. The parcel duly arrived, and was opened, and the horror of His Highness at the inspection of the contents was inconceivable. "Heavens! What have they sent me? Twelve human scalps with the skin on! How horrible! Where do the English get these scalps from? Do the English do these things? Away with them instantly!"

On another occasion half-a-dozen corded petticoats were sent for, and this gave as much cause for merriment at the expense of the poor Rajah as the first story. The idea of this item of the costume of a European female being required for the royal household of an Indian prince was most laughable, and must have astonished the Madras shopkeepers not a little. This puts me in mind of another anecdote, illustrative of native character and their business-like way of doing things. An officer was out shooting snipes, when firing at a bird, the contents of the gun unfortunately lodged in a native cooly, who, unperceived by the sportsman, was working in the field. Captain F. was not aware at the time of the extent of the mischief done, but it appears the wound proved fatal. Next day he was surprised to receive a deputation from the relatives of the deceased, who handed him a document, purporting to be a valuation of the deceased's life, and soliciting payment of the same, with a receipt for the amount demanded. This extraordinary document ran thus :—

Captain F.	Dr.
	Rupees.
To one bloody murder committed . .	5
Contents received.	

There's a tradesman-like way of doing business with a vengeance.

But I must return to my visit to His Highness. I was ushered upstairs after a moderate interval into the State apartments, where His Highness was sitting on a splendid couch. He rose to meet me, and gave me a seat at his right hand, the left not being so honourable. He talked English remarkably well, and asked me numberless questions upon a variety of subjects. After about half an hour, His Highness rose to dismiss me, for Eastern etiquette demands that the person who is visited should be the first to end an interview or visit, and it would be a breach of politeness and manners for a visitor to be the first to get up and go away. At a signal given, garlands of flowers were brought in on gold and silver trays, and I was covered with wreaths of highly-scented flowers, looking like a maypole on the first of May. Then His Highness took a bottle and sprinkled me with rose-water, deliciously cool and fragrant. I had now to perform a most difficult operation, which was to back out of the room, for I could not turn my back on royalty. By a series of bowing and scraping and crab-like manœuvres to this side and that side, I managed to steer clear of all obstacles and gain the door ; then stripping myself of my floral decoration, I jumped into my carriage and drove home.

My visit to the palace puts me in mind of an entertainment given some years ago by the Rajah of Tanjore, where there was an exhibition of the wrestlings of men and fights among half-wild animals. It may possess some interest as a characteristic picture of doings at a Native Court. Myself and some guests who were in my house were invited to attend at the Residency in full dress at a certain hour, where we should find carriages ready to convey us to the Palace. Precisely at eleven we rode up to the Residency where we found the company was beginning to assemble. Groups of officers in brilliant uniforms were pacing up and down, their swords dangling at their sides and crimson sashes swinging to and fro as they strutted along the terraced front of the mansion. Civilians of all ages in their more modest white and black apparel, mixing in singular contrast with the glitter and show of the military, and of natives, many of all castes and colours, who mingled in this living group. With dark red turbans gracefully folded over their heads to a degree of neatness that might have raised a sigh from Beau Brummell, with long garments white as the driven snow, with belts made from tiger or leopard skins thrown over their shoulders and fastened round the waist by a plate of highly polished silver or brass, with a short *crease* encased in a green velvet sheath, and coloured shawls carefully tied round the waist as a showy contrast to the extreme whiteness of their other garments; with all these decorations they formed by no means the least conspicuous objects in this motley gathering.

Immediately in front of the Residency were drawn up about eight or ten conveyances of a most questionable description, and which could not fail to raise a smile or sneer from the beholders. The most worthless hackney-coach in Oxford Street would have shone as a Lord Mayor's carriage in comparison with these strange antediluvian vehicles. It was the mustering of all the routiest, rustiest, queerest four-wheeled conveyances ever devised for the luxury or misery of man that made our procession from the Residency such a comical proceeding. In a filthy, old-fashioned chariot, coeval with Job, begrimed with dirt, and long ago a stranger to the slightest speck of paint either inside or out, cushionless and comfortless, might be seen the bright uniforms of two or three officers its unworthy occupants. We were going *in state*, and these were our *state* carriages. Then there was the coachman, the "smart" postboys, and "Jeames" on the dickey behind. My friend Wildman was standing near me. "These," he said with a smile, "are some of the luxuries of the East. This is a barouche. There's a landau. Here's a brougham, a cabriolet. Take your choice. And now look at the postboys, more original than the carriages or the horses they bestride." Leading me by the hand Wildman begged me to regard one of these curious descendants of Diomede whom he so facetiously styled the "smart" postboys. A native of the darkest hue, with a pair of dirty striped trousers, no shoes or stockings, a green threadbare jacket of old velvet, and to crown all *such* a hat, broken and battered to half its original dimensions, and of which the poorest son of Erin would scorn to be accused as the owner.

While thus indulging in free humour upon the carriages, horses, and drivers before us, I suddenly felt a tap on my shoulder, and turning round was addressed by the Resident, who said, "Will you choose a conveyance for yourself? We are about to start. With the exception of the foremost, you can choose any you see." Giving a hasty glance at the motley collection of indescribables before me, I fixed, without further delay, upon a capacious barouche, and jumping inside called to Wildman, who immediately followed after me, banging the rusty door with a crash that made the old vehicle rattle again.

And so we started, the Resident's carriage taking the lead and the other ones following at a pace which did more credit to the cattle than I was at first willing to assign them. Dashing out at the Residency gate we came at once in the native town, and there the whole stream of the populace was drawn up in two lines along the road, staring with astonishment and delight at the cavalcade that was passing before them. We had numerous outriders in the shape of natives of all descriptions, who displayed no little skill in horsemanship as they cantered past on their rough, unbroken horses or ponies. Others on foot kept tearing and rushing along endeavouring to keep pace with the rattling wheels, shouting, yelling, laughing, and jostling each other as they scampered onwards as if their very life depended upon their speedy arrival at the Palace Gate.

In about ten minutes we reached the outer gate of the Fort, and threading the rather intricate windings of the several gateways we at length got fairly inside, and after passing through two or three streets finally pulled up in front of the Palace.

To those who have been accustomed to regard Windsor Castle as the standard of a royal habitation, the picture I shall endeavour to pourtray of the exterior of the Palace of the Rajah of Tanjore will appear an amusing contrast. In the centre of a large and particularly dirty quadrangle, built in the midst of a populous city, a long wall defaced, half destroyed, and blackened by age and the mischief of the inhabitants, a tiled roof and a few apertures in the walls that do duty for windows, is the first sight of the Palace that greets the stranger's eye. A huge gateway, under which is an enormous massive gate with folding doors, stands in the centre of the building. A few miserable sentinels (I suppose I should call them household troops) with unwashed belts, threadbare coats, slovenly in appearance, and cased in pantaloons of every size and colour, sauntered idly under the great archway, looking like the ghosts of soldiers who had been posted there in the days of Tippoo and never been relieved since. Here, indeed, was the mere shadow of royalty and kingly authority, and looking at this spectacle, if such might be a criterion, who could be surprised that our own well-fed and well-disciplined sepoys knocked down the numerous hordes of Hyder and Tippoo even though ten to one, aye, and as Gibbon says the Turks did to the Chinese, " mowed them down like grass."

But in these reflections I was soon called away to move onwards, as all our party had alighted and were preparing to enter the Hall of Kings. It was some time before I could realise the fact that we were entering a palace, but my ideas of grandeur and state were soon dissipated, and I henceforth resolved to wonder at nothing, but to take everything as it came. And now what a scene ensued! Instead of being conducted by Guards of Honour to the Royal Presence, we were left, Resident included, to find our own way. The glittering uniforms of the officers had attracted to the spot crowds upon crowds of natives who completely hemmed us in on every side.

Forwards, backwards, on either side they stood around us like a field of standing corn. In vain the Peons endeavoured by their shoutings, threats, and gestures to keep back the growing multitude ; in vain the ghastly sentinels brought down their rusty muskets to the "charge," and thrust the people back with their blunted bayonets ; in vain were our own fists employed in dealing right and left the most desperate blows in self-defence ; in vain were unlucky heads belaboured with bamboos, sticks, and whips, the tide increased every moment, and we were finally hemmed in, became separated from each other, and lost among the multitude. Our object was to enter the narrow gateway, and so gain the inner court of the palace. Hopeless indeed seemed our struggle. Never were we so thoroughly helpless, yet still each individual pressed on as best he could to the goal.

Our height, our boots, and dogged resolution gave us great advantage over the small, naked-footed native, till finally by incredible efforts we emerged, breathless and wearied, out of the living crowd. Yet we came not all together, and those who issued first had at least the satisfaction—poor consolation—of welcoming the safety of the rest, till at last we all met again, having been pushed out more by the force of the moving mass than by any single vigorous efforts of our own. When I think of it all at this day, I wonder I am alive to tell the story.

The scene which now presented itself was one of a truly oriental character. We entered a spacious open court, the sides of which were occupied by galleries filled with men and women, whose coloured dresses, glittering ornaments, richly decorated turbans and sparkling jewels composed a most attractive spectacle as they sat, eager with expectation, in their dense ranks one above the other.

The scene before us appeared the realisation of the Arabian nights, so thoroughly Eastern was it in every respect. The hum and whisperings of the breathing crowds appeared to relax as we entered the court, and we had no sooner advanced a few paces before a richly dressed native official (the Dewan or Prime Minister I presume) approached the Resident and conducted him to an elevated platform decorated with festoons of flowers and hung with superbly embroidered tapestry. In the centre of the dais was the royal throne, and chairs and ottomans were arranged on both sides for the accommodation of the English visitors and officials. As we each ascended one after the other, we were formally introduced to His Highness, who shaking us by the hand with much cordiality of manner, presented us each with a beautiful nosegay, hanging a garland of flowers round our neck at the same time, the perfume from which was much heightened by a quantity of rose-water, which had previously been sprinkled over them. Thus adorned, we were commanded (in kingly phrase) to sit down, and the Rajah seating himself on the Musnud we seated ourselves, some on the right and others on the left of His Highness. Behind the throne were the members of the Royal Family (all standing up), consisting of about seven or eight persons, varying in age from fourscore to fifteen. From the elevated station where we were, we were enabled to take a general survey of all around and below us, and gazing upon the brilliant spectacle I would dare to say that the thousands of eyes that looked in our direction were for a time entirely fixed upon our group, for in whatever direction I cast my eyes I met the united gaze of hundreds of men, women, and children darting their looks of surprise or delight at the small handful of Englishmen that now sat with their pale faces and scarlet and lace coats round the throne of the Rajah.

Immediately below us was the arena where presently were exhibited the sports and pastimes of this eventful day. After a brief interval one of the Rajah's attendants made the sign to begin. Perfectly unconscious of what was about to take place, I leant gently over the railing in front, and observing a stir among the crowd, soon guessed the quarter from whence the sport would commence. In a moment the crowd gave way on both sides, and suddenly rushed forward two burly men, who coming up at a smart pace entered an enclosure in the arena, and advancing in front of the throne prostrated themselves three successive times before the Rajah. Their arms, head, and feet were uncovered, but they had a cloth firmly tied round the waist, and thus appeared to all intents and purposes braced up for a contest. These men were called "Jetties," and a certain number of them are kept and fed like wild beasts, by Hindoo Rajahs, and on festive occasions are brought out to display their barbarous feats before the assembled guests. A small strip of hardened hide or piece of Bamboo is tied round the joints of their middle fingers, and on this are four sharp edges, something similar to the Roman cæstus. Armed solely with these, the Jetties engage in single combat, and so keen are the edges of the "cæstus," that the slightest blow is sufficient to draw blood.

The object of the combatants is to try which can wound his adversary most severely, and thus offer the most bloody spectacle to the Rajah's eyes. But both conquerer and conquered receive a present at the end of the exhibition, and in the event of death succeeding this frightful tragedy (which not unfrequently happens), the family of the deceased is provided for by the state: and thus it is that men will not hesitate to display for the gratification of a barbarous king one of the most disgusting exhibitions that ever disgraced humanity. The fight seldom lasts more than a few moments. The wretched men soon grapple and close. You see their eager hands endeavouring by sheer force to avert the dreadful wound which the spikes will cause. You see the struggle—a painful struggle, as if life itself were at stake—you watch the angry countenance—the rising wrath, the desperate, yet often fruitless, attempt to deal the fatal blow, till suddenly there is an ominous pause, and then you discern the blood slowly trickling down the forehead of one of the combatants, and that one, regardless of his sufferings, now more fiercely presses forward, more madly grapples to take his revenge. With one vigorous effort he wrests away his adversary's right arm, which has hitherto been firmly clenched round his own, and concentrating all his remaining strength into one single blow, he aims at the forehead of his antagonist, and thrusting the cæstus into the flesh, he tears it along in the bitterness of his own agony and the sweetness of revenge, over the whole length of the head as far as the neck, literally dividing the flesh to the very bone, like a plough over the unfurrowed field, causing the blood to run over both victor and vanquished. I turned almost sick at contemplating this sight, so degrading to humanity, but now it was over, and I looked up at the Rajah's countenance to see if I could observe any expression of satisfaction at witnessing a scene fraught with so much barbarity and horror. He was pleasantly talking to his courtiers, perhaps applauding the issue of the combat, and in a voice of mild authority he ordered a second couple to be brought into the lists. Again were we doomed to witness a repetition of the same, nor until ten or twelve rounds had been exhibited was there any change in the royal amusements.

Other feats succeeded these, among which was one which especially attracted my attention, as it certainly exhibited great skill in the performer. A man came upon the stage armed from head to foot with keen-edged knives of various shapes and sizes. They were tied on, about five or six on each arm, a similar number on each of his calves and feet, pointed, fearful-looking weapons whose very touch would draw blood. Thus encased in a rampart of sharp blades, he skipped about and threw himself into every imaginable attitude, flinging up his legs, twisting and turning his arms a thousand ways—right, left, backwards, forwards, it appearing to the spectator at every movement that at least one of the knives must have pierced his flesh somewhere. But so dexterously did he manage his evolutions that, though for quite an hour he was constantly throwing himself into every fantastic shape conceivable, yet he did not allow his skin to be grazed in the slightest degree. The poor fellow, at last, was thoroughly fatigued after all his exertions, and then came to make his salaam to the Rajah and withdrew; and so he played his part.

But if the two spectacles I have described were barbarous and frightful to behold, the next, ludicrous as it was, has puzzled me ever since in thinking how it was managed. A boy of about ten years old was brought in who, to the astonishment of all beholders, sat upon his own head! It was a startling performance. By some inexplicable method of contorting his body he certainly accomplished his object, and no sooner was he fairly settled (and perhaps comfortably) than he began moving about and round and round in a most droll manner. I conclude that the extreme suppleness of the limbs of children allows them to twist themselves into any imaginable shape, and probably practice from their tenderest years facilitates the accomplishment of what otherwise would be a matter of impossibility. We know, too, that all Orientals can twist their limbs to a degree impracticable to a European; and so it is that, by nature and constant practice, these supple natives can attain the unenviable distinction of being able to make a chair of their own pericranium.

Last of all came the fightings of the animals, and though these were less shocking to behold than those of human-kind, yet they, too, were not unmixed with cruelty. Two enormous buffaloes were first led into the arena, being kept in a half wild state purposely for these exhibitions. Each was led by its own native keeper by means of a cord passed through the nostrils, that part of the animal being so highly sensitive that a child might lead and check one of the fiercest. Previous to loosening the cord by which they were held, they were allowed to approach each other face to face; again they were drawn back, and a second, third, and fourth time permitted to come near again. This was done to excite them, and generate such ferocity as would ensure a grand combat. Suddenly, at a given signal, the keepers let slip the cord, and rushed to the door to make a hasty escape, while the buffaloes, free and left to themselves, gazed at each other with looks of rage and savage grandeur, yet each apparently unwilling to commence the deadly strife. At last the bolder of the two makes a move; his antagonist watches his very eye, they gaze at each other for an instant, they both retreat backwards as far as the sides of the arena will permit, and then, both making a violent bound forward, come with full force, their heads lowered one directly against the other, their foreheads being the immediate point of contact. The shock is so powerful that the huge brutes recoil at the blow, and, again retiring to the walls of the enclosure, again and again repeat the attack, till at last, one of them being overpowered and fatigued by a succession of such formidable blows, gives up the contest, and as his antagonist rushes on again, he as suddenly slips to one side, while his adversary, not expecting that no resistance would be offered to his head-thrust, loses his equilibrium, trips over, and comes right down on his knees or nose, or tumbles completely over. Enraged at being thus dealt with, the excited beast rises as quickly as possible, and chasing his vanquished foe round the arena, endeavours to pierce him with his horns in the ribs. Thus they both run wild and furious, one after the other, the pursued bellowing with all his might, and the pursuer occasionally, as he reaches his flying enemy, giving him the most frightful gashes with his horns, until the latter at last drops down exhausted and overcome. The buffaloes are then led away, and afterwards rams, antelopes, and other horned animals are exhibited in the same manner; but none of these afforded a sight equal to that of the buffaloes. The last of all was a wild boar and a goat; but the latter animal, in order to possess a defensive advantage equal to the tushes of the boar, had a long sharp knife tied to its forehead, and whenever it charged and butted the boar, it of necessity ran this knife into the ribs of the latter. Thus the strife was equalized, and gave the goat so great an advantage, that nine times out of ten it came out the victor.

This was the closing scene, the Resident signifying to the Rajah that we were now anxious to depart. We all arose. The Rajah standing up, shook each of us by the hand as we passed before him, the Resident remaining at his right side, and telling our names and rank as we successively came forward. More flowers and garlands were showered upon us, until we appeared to bear upon our shoulders the whole produce of a garden. As soon as we had reached the outer court, we at once divested ourselves of our floral decorations, and each made the best of his way to search out his vehicle. But lo! what a change! Instead of barouches and cabriolets, we found seven or eight large elephants mounted with howdahs, and caparisoned with scarlet cloths and other trappings. All appeared done with the wand of a genie. However, we proceeded to choose our elephant, licensed to carry four outside. I suggested a ladder, when a mahout, or driver, came up and asked if we were ready to mount. Replying in the affirmative, he speedily solved all difficulties about mounting. "Take care, sahib, stand aside," and saying this, he gently tapped the elephant's knee with a small cane, speaking at the same time a word or two to the sagacious animal. The obedient beast instantly knelt down at the command of its master, bringing its huge body as far down as it possibly could to the level of our heads. By a succession of steps, during which I traversed the whole of one leg, a part of the side, the head, and a portion of the back, I gradually reached the top, and seized the howdah firmly. Meanwhile, Wildman and the others had crawled over the opposite side of the animal, and we all met simultaneously at the summit, congratulating each other on our safe arrival. When we had taken our places in the howdah, the mahout cried out, "Now, gentlemen, take care. Catch tight hold of the sides of the howdah. The elephant is going to rise, and if you don't look out you'll be thrown right over his head." Consoling words to us who seemed already to be on the brink of destruction, and had now the chance of being pitched into the gulf. We firmly grasped the howdah with both hands. The mahout spoke a word: the elephant rose up, and at the same time communicated to us a motion indescribable in its feeling, and to which nothing bears comparison. It was a mixture of violent jerks, upwards, forwards, and backwards, all taking place, as it were, simultaneously, and had we not been previously warned to "catch hold" it is most certain we should have got down much quicker than we had got up.

We now moved off in procession on our return to the Residency. Some were clamorous for a race, but the elephants had no idea of being made racehorses, and in spite of all attempts one refused to pass the other. Besides, as we were going through the crowded streets, we should have trampled half the populace under foot. I never experienced anything so distressing and disagreeable as that ride. We did not go out of an ordinary trot, but that was the trot of an elephant, and was sufficient, nor do I think I could ever be induced to undertake such a ride again.

CHAPTER IV.

Trichore — Elephant traps — Sport in the Jungles— Mulliatoor—Expedition across the Cochin Mountains —Return to Trevandrum—Dewan Madava Rao— Adoption.

OUR stay in the capital this time did not extend beyond a few days, and we were soon off again towards Cochin. Our first halting-place was Quilon, properly Collam, signifying in Malyalum a tank. It was built A.D. 825, and was at one time a place of considerable importance. The natives of the country begin their era from its foundation, in the same manner as the natives of Cochin begin theirs from the origin of the Island of Vaipeen. In former days there were a great many weaving-looms and manufactories of cotton and stone-ware here. An excellent fortress was built here by Alexius Menezes, the first Archbishop of Goa, but being neglected by the

Dutch it soon fell into ruin. Marco Polo, who lived in the fourteenth century, gives perhaps the earliest accounts of Quilon, especially alluding to the manufacture of Indigo which was then carried on here.* It is slightly so at the present day, though on a very reduced scale. Lace is still made here. It certainly, from all accounts, was a place of considerable trade in earlier days, but now the shadow only exists. A regiment of Native Infantry is stationed here. Midway between Trevandrum and Quilon is another dismantled fortress, built by the Dutch, at a place now known as Anjengo, a corruption of two Tamil words, *Unjee Taynkul*, the five cocoa palms. Here for many years was an English Factory, and indeed it was a place of commercial importance in former days. It is now desolate and deserted. The ruins of the Portuguese Church still exist. Robert Orme, the historian of Hindostan, was born here. Educated at Harrow, he became a Member of Council at Madras, and died in England at the age of seventy-three. Another celebrity was born here, Mrs. Elizabeth Draper, wife of one

* See Marco Polo's Travels, p. 410. Bohn's Ed.

of the Councillors at Surat, and to whom Sterne addressed the well-known "Letters to Eliza." She lies buried at Bristol.

After a fortnight's residence at Cochin we went on to Trichore, where I anticipated much sport in the jungles. Here I resume my journal.

February 2nd.—The Conservator of forests and myself left Trichore at an early hour in palanquins, leaving the young Rajah to follow at his own time, he having expressed a desire to see some sport. We proposed spending four or five days at Palapillay, a station in the heart of the jungle, abounding with large game. Arriving at a river about daylight, where we had previously sent our horses to await us, we soon crossed, and resting a short time for the purpose of loading our guns, we struck at once into the forest, disturbing in their solitudes numbers of pea-fowl and jungle-fowl. Reached the camp about eight o'clock. This is indeed a wild spot. The dwelling we reside in is the Conservator's office, a thatched building with mud walls. Close by is a large elephant cage, where those animals after capture are kept for four months, to be educated and to undergo all the processes of taming. We breakfast in the verandah, dine under the trees, and sleep secure from wild animals in a dark, gloomy apartment hedged off on one side of the building. There is a small open space in front, and everywhere else is jungle, jungle.

After breakfast we awaited the arrival of the Rajah, who had gone to a Pagoda some five miles off to perform certain daily religious ceremonies which could on no account be dispensed with. One of His Highness's objects in coming here was to see a wild elephant which had lately been caught in a trap, the original invention of the Conservator, who planned and constructed it himself. It consists of a large piece of ground of an oblong shape enclosed by huge trunks of trees cut and branched for the purpose, and placed upright in the ground at a distance of a foot or more apart. These are connected again with transverse beams, rendering the place very strong and secure against escape. At each end are two large doors held up by a cable running over the centre of the enclosure, and which, being brought over a pulley, is tied to a thick slip of wood placed across the centre of the trap. The bait consists of about 200 plaintain trees, which are well watered and kept green for the purpose. The length of the trap is about seventy yards, and its breadth about fifteen yards. The elephants enter for the purpose of eating the plaintain trees, and as they go on they touch the cross-beam with their head, which when knocked down loosens the cable and the doors fall at both ends, and Mr. Elephant is then left to finish his meal at leisure. Should the animal chance to break down the piles or logs of which the sides of the trap are composed, even then he could not escape, for around the outside are dug pits some twenty feet deep, into which he would of necessity fall if he attempted to rush away. K. had succeeded in capturing a large male elephant in this novel trap, and when we saw it it had become nearly tame. It is now employed as a call-bird, for K. is most sanguine about entrapping an entire herd before long. The Rajah, who was with us, was much pleased with everything. Afterwards K. and myself partook of some cocoanut milk and cold tea, but the Rajah, whose religious scruples forbade him to touch a drop of anything without previously bathing, was deploring the heat and consequent thirst.

"I feel the fatigue so much the more," he said, "as I am not allowed to drink anything." To which I jokingly replied that it was an opportunity to leave off such customs entailing such discomfort. He said nothing, but walked on, the picture of misery and exhaustion, evidently very desirous of his ablutions and a good draught of some liquid restorative.

I had shot an elk on our way, and coming home separated from the rest of the party, and took a byepath in the hopes of falling in with some large game. I soon fell in with a herd of bison feeding on the side of the hill. But they soon saw me, and at first stood as if they were preparing to rush at and crush me. However, they gradually began to move off. I took a steady aim at one of them, when there was such a crash through the jungle that the place must have swarmed with them. They passed in single file before me till I thought the line would never end, and though I was unable to count them, I am sure there must have been fifty or more in that herd. I think I never saw so much game as I did to-day. Counting everything, I saw twenty-one peacocks, nine jungle-fowl, seven elk, and two herds of bison. I had altogether fifteen shots, made some good bags, and was out till dusk. I mention this for the benefit of those who may hereafter be fortunate enough to find themselves in the neighbourhood of those "happy hunting grounds."

4th.—Sat up till late on the banks of a river expecting a tiger to come and drink. I was ensconced behind a temporarily erected defence of bushes, from whence I could fire on my victim without being seen. But the night wore on—no thirsty tiger came my way, and I was preparing to return homewards, when I heard the voice of a jolly traveller come pouring down through the jungle, and along he came in the dry course of the stream singing and bellowing with all his might, evidently for the purpose of scaring away any wild animal that might cross his path, and that he was a "vacuus viator," entitled to sing even before robbers. As he had probably spoilt our sport by his noisy melodies, we thought to frighten him by suddenly roaring out like a tiger as soon as he came opposite our quarters. The poor fellow was sadly dismayed for the moment. He threw away his stick, and stood trembling for an instant as if he was going to be devoured the next. But his fear was only momentary, and going on his way he said, "Ah! you are only sportsmen, sitting there to kill bison."

6th.—This morning the Resident joined us. Palapillay never had such distinguished and such numerous company since the days of Tippoo. The natives were in a state of wild excitement, especially the Mulchers or Hill Coolies, who expressed great surprise at "seeing white men come to eat and drink in such manner." Some of Tippoo's horsemen encamped in this very spot, and the inhabitants still talk of those days with horror, for they were sadly ill-used by the wanton soldiery; their goods stolen, houses destroyed, and shops sacked and ravaged. Though this is only now an insignificant village, consisting of a few huts in the very centre of a dense forest, yet it is certain that formerly where is now jungle there were numerous habitations, and that other villages were scattered far in the interior, now occupied by wild beasts. Traces of houses and entire villages prove this, and now it would appear that man is once more asserting his power over these desolate and deserted tracts, and for the second time industry and civilization are pushing on with improvements and blessings into the wildest recesses of the forest. Every scrap of land that lies low between the surrounding hills is now converted into rice cultivation. The elephants have notice to quit, and to prove how vast a change has taken place with regard to the clearing of jungle land during the last twenty years, there used to be a famous "beat" for tigers where the Missionary Church at Trichore now stands, and the tank close to the Commandant's house, which is now resorted to by the villagers for washing clothes and bathing, used to be the chief drinking-place at night of the wild animals. Three miles from Palapillay there is a remarkable collection of Cromlechs on a rocky hill, in the heart of the thickest forest. How, when, and by whom they were erected I leave others to determine. I went to see them, and exceedingly curious they were. The Mulchers know nothing of them traditionally, though they regard them with superstitious awe and reverence. They do not claim them as burying places of their ancestors, for their mode of sepulture is altogether different. In fact they know nothing about them. Who does? This has been real "life in the jungle" the last few days, and I would not change it for all the gaiety and bustle and conventionalities of London or Leamington. Here we are free to go and to do what we like. We have every needful comfort, luxury and liberty. No game-laws, no turnpikes, no taxes, no trespass. Here we have no need of silk waistcoats, or pumps, or other preparations for a formal dinner-party.

We dress and dine in sporting costume, not the less neat or clean for all that, and, with the table spread under a tree, dispatch with the greatest pleasure a brace of jungle-fowl, or a bison's tongue, or elk chops—all glorious dishes in their way; and then, in default of stronger liquor, what can be more grateful or wholesome than cocoanut milk and wild honey, with the bees still lingering and dying in their own sweetness. Parents have no occasion to lament over their poor boy who has gone to India. This said pitied youngster is often more rich and happy than those he left behind, if he will only be true to himself. The physical diseases we suffer from are not so fatal as those moral diseases we bring upon ourselves. India has unquestionably many advantages, and is not in the main unhealthy. Exercise and temperance must be studied, but I have besides often observed that the most active-minded have best resisted the climate.

11th.—Rode five miles to Annanuddy through a wild and beautiful part of the country. We are encamped on the banks of a river where the elephants appear to have been enjoying themselves mightily in the water. After dinner rode out about four miles with my gun. I had only an hour of daylight left, for it was past five o'clock, so I made the coolies run as fast as their legs could carry them, so as to have at least one shot before sunset. I was fortunate in securing one jungle-cock. While beating a small patch of jungle, four elk most unexpectedly rose up before me, and trotted off quite leisurely at the distance of fifteen paces. I gave them a volley of small shot—very unsportsmanlike, I admit—but *cui bono?* They only laughed at me, and trotted on. It was quite dark when I left off beating, and I was four miles from the tents; but I trusted to the horse's sagacity to find his way over a very rough and broken road, never drawing rein till I reached the river. So in about an hour and a half I had ridden eight miles, walked about three, and had seen four elks, eight or nine snipes, two hares, and five jungle-fowl. Such is sport out here, unhampered by game laws or certificates.

14th.—Rode ten miles to Alwaye. We crossed two rivers in boats, and are now encamped on the Alwaye river. This is the famous spa watering-place of Cochin, from which place we are fourteen miles. The Cochinites flock here for bathing in the season, the waters having the doubtful reputation of healing every kind of disease. I have at present no bodily ailment whereby I could test the efficacy of this miraculous stream, but I must trust it will act as a preventive against future complaints, for I plunge in and take a glorious swim every morning before breakfast. Alligators abound here, but only in the deep pools; yet Mr. Owen, a resident here, was bathing opposite his house the other morning, when, according to his own declaration, his nose came suddenly in contact with a huge alligator, which has had such an effect upon his nerves that he has not had the courage to enter the water since.

Friday, 16th Feb.—I was up at three this morning, and set off in a canoe for the purpose of making an expedition up the river to a place about fifteen miles off. My skiff was very small, and I could only lie down lengthwise at the bottom, having previously had a leafy covering put over the mattress to protect me from the sun's rays. I had four paddlers and a servant. Numerous sand banks and flats obstructed my progress—so much so, that at daylight I found I had only gone six miles. The boatmen had repeatedly to get out and drag the canoe a long way over flats where there was not half a foot of water. However, we manfully persevered, determined to overcome all difficulties. I was so much absorbed in contemplating the beautiful scenery on either side, and the distant mountains covered with forest, looking so fair and so refreshing, that I almost regretted our labours ended about eleven o'clock, when after seven hours I at last reached Mulliatoor. It is a very pretty spot, and has a small bungalow built on a high bank overlooking the stream. The river here bends suddenly to the right, and is soon lost to sight in the dark forests that come down to the water's edge. In the extreme distance is a group of lofty hills, forming a most picturesque background to so lovely a landscape, and covered with dense forest, from whose unexplored recesses come silently streaming on the clear blue waters of the river. How I longed to explore the river to its very source, whose fountains are probably known only to the tiger or elephant, and perhaps too darkly concealed even from them!

It is a constant and common complaint, yet a true one, that so much time is idly thrown away by young men in this country. But wherein lies the fault? If every young officer had received the groundwork of a military education before leaving England, or had even the advantages of a year's study after his arrival, he would in nine cases out of ten imbibe a taste for study and employment which would never desert him. There should be minor institutions at the principal stations of the army, where books and instruments might be available and lent out, and so a direct encouragement given to those who had any taste for the scientific parts of their profession. There might also be museums established in each district, under the charge of the collector and engineer, for the collection of geological specimens, botany, or any branch of natural history, and thus in various ways many kinds of employment and occupation suited to individual tastes might be opened to young men who now, in default of anything of the kind, have the alternative of the billiard-room, or otherwise idling away the days and hours without any resource tending to improve their minds or elevate their character. " How often," remarked the Resident to me one day (and he has been in India half a century), "have I regretted through life in this country that I was never taught a *little* music or a *little* drawing before I came out."

But in spite of the deficiency of the education he lives to lament, General C. has, nevertheless, not allowed the abilities with which Nature has gifted him to run to waste. He is a rare instance of a superior mind struggling against great disadvantages, and attaining eminence through his own diligence and perseverance. Education he had none at school, and with all his self-accumulated knowledge he laments the poverty of his parents, who were unable to afford him the minor accomplishments of a little drawing and music. How many there are who come out here having received a brilliant education both at school and at college, but when once launched upon the idle ocean of Indian life, abandon all their acquirements for fleeting and unintellectual pleasures, and neglect those useful arts which they might turn to so good account, and a smattering of which really great and wise men in other respects would sacrifice half their present luxuries to obtain.

Tuesday, 6th.—His Highness the Rajah having expressed his intention of coming to pay the Resident a visit this afternoon, preparations were made to give him a suitable reception.

The escort of twenty-four Sepoys were drawn up in readiness to receive him on landing, which he would do at a small jetty running out into the water. At the appointed hour we descried the Rajah coming across in his boat, a two-masted sailing boat built at Cochin, and accompanying him was a cabin boat with fourteen rowers, having a sofa on the top covered with purple velvet and gold fringe. On landing the guard presented arms, and the Resident conducted His Highness to chairs arranged for the purpose. Shortly after, an addition was made to the party by the arrival of one of the young princes, who happened to be sailing about in his pleasure boat. When the Resident saw who it was, he immediately despatched a boat with swift rowers to summon him to the audience. His brother tried to make excuses for him, saying he was not in costume. "Oh! hang the dress; let him come," urged the Resident. So in a few minutes he arrived at the jetty and came ashore; but before landing, he stepped aboard his brother's larger vessel, and suddenly dived down into the cabin to see if he could find some royal garments to clothe himself withal. Presently he issued forth from below like a fresh grasshopper, with a green silk skull-cap and green gown to match, and I should say, from the expression on his countenance, he rather felt the unpleasantness of appearing in borrowed plumes to which he was not accustomed. Our little durbar lasted about an hour, when the royal visitors once more embarked and sailed away.

March 20th.—Having got information that an elephant had been playing his pranks at a village near Trichore for the last three or four days, I made preparations for a trip there, in hopes of securing the destroyer and avenging the villagers, although it was distant from this about fifty miles. Leaving this by boat at 3 P.M., I went the first twenty miles by water, and thenceforward by land. The first day was occupied in gathering all the information I could respecting the vagaries of this troublesome animal, and feeling now assured of his existence and locality, I set out, and on the 26th was up before daylight and rode seven miles into the interior of the jungle, accompanied by two guides and my own three followers. About seven o'clock I reached the banks of a small river, running through a very thick bamboo jungle, and here it was that my guides beckoned me to dismount and sit down while they went to reconnoitre. After waiting about half an hour, I got tired at the delay, and resolved to go and look out for myself. Our course lay through the wide rocky bed of a mountain torrent, now dry, through an almost impenetrable forest, and after about a mile of this, we ascended a hill so steep and stony that I was forced to sit down constantly to regain my breath. I was in hopes that when we had reached the summit our labours would have been rewarded with a sight of the game. But we persevered, and ascended another eminence, and arrived at a cool shady spot, and there at last we came upon the tracks. "See!" said the guide, "they were here last night," and he had scarcely spoken ere I heard the crash of a bough a short way off, and made sure we were upon them. But all again became silent, so we determined to follow the tracks till we came upon them. We had not gone far when we came up with our game. There was one large tusker feeding quietly about sixty yards off, and this was the only one I saw at first; so I got behind a neighbouring tree, that I might take a survey of the position, and endeavour to get as near as possible without being seen. Immediately in front of me was what I thought was a large rock ; so I resolved to get behind the rock, and then if possible to another tree beyond, and so on till I came to suitable distance for taking a certain and steady aim. So I was on the point of running to get behind the rock, when to my inconceivable astonishment it began to move, and before I could understand what was taking place an enormous elephant, with as fine a pair of tusks as I ever saw, rose up and stood in front of me. I had not a moment to lose, and raising my gun fired at his head. He swerved round and paused an instant, as if uncertain of purpose. Though stunned by the shock, he seemed to throw a glance of revenge at the tree where my shot came from, but before he had time to consider that discretion was the better part of valour I gave him the second barrel, which determined him at once, for off he trotted, to my great and lasting disappointment. However, I followed him up. On he went, crashing and knocking down the trees and bushes in his course, and away I ran after him, up and down hill, and over rocks and fallen bushes. Every now and then I came up to him, and expected and hoped he would turn round and show fight, for I was well prepared to receive his attack, and he was grievously wounded. But he led me such a chase I was fain to give in from fatigue. From scouts I afterwards sent out, it appears the ground was strewn with gore in every direction.*

April 12th.—Set out this morning with the Resident on an expedition to the Nelliamputty Hills, for the purpose of deciding a boundary dispute between the British and Cochin Governments. The road—no, I am wrong, there was no road; but our route lay through thick jungles where no villages existed, and where the only trace of a path was along the smuggler's track, dim, uncertain, and changeable. We were accompanied by the Dewan and his son, and the Conservator of Forests, and our marching establishment consisted in all of some 300 people. For all these hungry mouths it was

* This elephant was found dead near the spot I had left him about two weeks afterwards. The tusks had been stolen, or I might have had a trophy after all.

necessary to carry food with us or starve. Consequently orders were given for twelve days' supplies of rice and other grain to be got ready for the natives, while we took poultry, sheep, and other necessaries for ourselves, not omitting a dozen she-goats with their kids for our milk supply. Our first day's march was to Mulliatoor, a place I have previously described as the limit of civilized life in these parts. The evening we arrived here there was a great festival at the Roman Catholic church on the opposite side of the river, and on the morrow (I was glad to think after our departure from the neighbourhood) there were to assemble there for the occasion some twenty to thirty thousand people. After dinner K. and I took a canoe and rowed over to the church, where we heard music and merry-making. The priests were very civil and obliging, showing us over the church, and paying us other kindly attentions. We ascertained they had got the band up from Cochin, consisting of about a dozen fiddles, a large drum, a tambourine, flageolet, &c., so instead of monopolizing all the melody to ourselves, I proposed to borrow the band for half an hour, take it across the water, and give the Resident a share in the fun. The musicians were delighted at the idea, and in five minutes we were all crowded in the boat and rowing across the stream to the tune of the "British Grenadiers." The Resident was delighted at our game, and kept the band playing for an hour or more; and on their going away, gave them a handsome present of ten rupees—a great windfall for them, and as much as they got elsewhere in as many weeks.

14th.—We were off at daylight, the Resident in his palanquin, while K. and I walked, having our guns in hand and ponies following. We followed a small pathway in the dense jungle for several miles, and it was nine o'clock before we reached the encampment, which was pitched, in default of a better locality, on the banks of a nearly dried-up mountain stream, the water running over a shallow, rocky bottom, with several deep pools at intervals. Below us was an enormous ledge of rock, over which the water fell in a cascade of 150 feet. During the monsoon this must be a magnificent waterfall, and the surrounding wildness of the scenery must, in unison with it, make up a grand scene at that season of the year. The name of this spot was Uddrapullay, and the miserable associations connected with it will long be retained in my memory, for, about four in the afternoon, there came on such a storm ot rain that, with our indifferent shelter, it rendered us very uncomfortable. Dinner was unavoidably postponed, the tents all leaked, the coolies ran away, and altogether so great was our discomfort in every particular that night that I was glad next morning when our tents were struck and we were off. Every further step we took we appeared to enter more dense jungle, where the thickness of the foliage must ever forbid the rays of the sun to penetrate. The fresh tracks of elephants continually crossed our path, and I could scarcely restrain my eagerness to follow after them. But who could say if I should be able to emerge again in safety from those gloomy, unknown, pathless recesses?

15th.—We arrived at Annacassum, and pitched the tents on the banks of a dry river-bed, fortunately finding just clear space enough for our accommodation. The "multitude" encamped in the bed of the river. At night we had relay guards of coolies to keep up an incessant shouting and howling to scare away the wild animals; for we were in the midst of their haunts, and could not see thirty yards before us in any direction. We halted here the next day to enable the elephants to bring up the tents, which had become very heavy from yesterday's rain. The next morning I took a guide and went to look for game, and at one time got close to an elephant, but he heard me and made off. The same evening I heard another crashing the bamboos not a mile from camp, but had no chance of getting near him, as it was growing dusk.

17th.—A short march to Oorcumbanaad. The tappal (postman) was met on the road by a herd of elephants, and had to climb and sleep up in a tree, being afraid to proceed till daylight.

18th.—Seven miles to Erapoory. After dinner I went out to look for game, and shot a bison as he was coming, unawares, to feed on the top of the hill where I was sitting.

The country begins to assume a more open appearance.

19th.—To Nellamputty. Here the forest ceases to be so uniformly dense, and large open tracks covered with patches of jungle, and large trees scattered here and there with a very park-like appearance, present a more pleasing landscape than what we have been accustomed to during the past few days. It commenced raining violently before our tents could come up, and we had some difficulty in keeping ourselves dry by seeking shelter under the lofty trees and a few native umbrellas. We halted here a day, and I found some employment for my gun with several herds of deer and bison.

The latter gave me a long chase one evening, but being caught in a heavy thunderstorm I gave up the pursuit.

21st.—We encamped on the edge of a very deep ravine. In the Himalaya they would call it a *khud*, and deep below we could hear a torrent rattling over the stones. I would not have been a somnambulist that night for something. It was three steps and overboard. We amused ourselves with rolling huge rocks over the precipice and listening to the awful crash they made as they resounded in their progress to the valley beneath. This place was called Manjeepara.

22nd.—This morning we ascended a steep hill which, from its summit, commanded a glorious landscape of the mountainous country we had just passed through. We were surrounded by hills on all sides, but our panorama extended fourteen or fifteen miles at least. Here we erected a hut to take our breakfast in; after which we pushed on for six more miles, again encamping on the edge of a steep precipice, far more fearful to look at than the last. But our situation was nevertheless a charming one, for we had a view of the low country stretching even to the sea, where we could plainly distinguish a vessel in the roads at Chowghaut, about fifteen miles off. It now began to rain furiously, and the fog was so thick we could not see each other's tents, nor was it before three o'clock that the mist cleared off and displayed a sudden descent into a valley at our feet, and a lofty mountain rising abruptly on the other side. This latter is called Pothindoo —the highest peak in the range—about 4,500 ft. above the sea level. We halted here a day, but the cold and rain were so intense, that all the kids and half the goats died in the night. We had, however, opened a communication with the low country, and therefore had no occasion to despair at our loss, for supplies came in to-day sufficient for all parties, and the coolies had no longer to exist on half rations. While the wind was at its highest, I was talking outside my tent to a native functionary on the prospects of the weather, and was amused by his remarks about "this fellow" the boisterous wind. While shivering painfully in the cold he delivered himself of this charming piece of philosophy: "This wind," says he, "he never stop still. The sun rest; the moon rest; sometimes the sea rest; but this fellow he never rest." Poor old man. This restless fellow appeared to drive through and through him as he uttered these words.

24th.—We descended the pass this morning, and breakfasted in the dry bed of a river at the foot, a romantic spot, and afterwards rode on to a village where we put up in a thatched barn, the first comfortable roof we had enjoyed for nearly three weeks. A few miles ride further brought us to Neemary, where we were lodged in a native dwelling-house, with just enough accommodation to keep us dry. Still we pushed on till we came, in the heart of the jungle, to a shed with open sides, exactly like a pound for cattle, and here we managed to spend the day, till about five in the evening we set off for Trichore. We were all glad when this mountain expedition was over. In five days after our return the Resident was laid up with fever, and I took a holiday to Coimbatore.

Soon after my return to Trevandrum, I went down one evening to pay a private visit to His Highness the Rajah. He received me in a kind of state apartment, a long room filled with tables covered with all kinds of ornaments and knick-knacks, and with the walls crammed with large mirrors and old-fashioned pictures. I entered by the large front door, and His Highness came out of a small recess at the other end of the room. He was dressed in a short green silk jacket, red silk trousers, and a brocaded skull-cap. He was somewhat corpulent in appearance, and in manners most affable and courteous. We seated ourselves and began chatting away, while every now and then he would empty the contents of his mouth upon the floor (the custom of the country I conclude), which said contents were produced at a rapidly increasing rate by the quid of Betel which he was chewing all the time. Every now and then an attendant in waiting brought him a brass vessel, out of which taking a draught of water he would more thoroughly rinse out his throat and scatter the blackened fluid all over the matting. This was the only disagreeable part of my visit; but I suppose it is all excusable in Royalty. With his conversation and kind manners I was much gratified, and when he asked me after a short interval whether I should like to see his children, I replied that nothing would give me greater pleasure. A messenger was forthwith despatched to the nursery to ask mamma to let the little ones come down, and in a few moments the small fry made their appearance. I may say without exaggeration that I seldom met a more interesting-looking youth than the eldest boy, a lad of about ten years old. He is very fair, with an intelligent countenance. He seemed so good and amiable, and talked English exceedingly well. He was dressed in a scarlet frock, embroidered with gold lace, on his head was a brocaded cap, beneath which his jet black hair made a striking and beautiful contrast with his charming features. The next was a boy about four or five years younger, and the third, a little girl, in whom papa seemed to take especial interest and pride. After shaking hands with the pet of the nursery, I discovered to my horror that she was suffering from a cutaneous malady, a fact which her callous parent subsequently brought to my notice, when I replied, "Yes, I observed it before," and thought to myself what a precious plight for a princess to be in! But the great delight of the Rajah was to show to visitors how well his little daughter could read English. Having got a book he opened it and told the little girl (she was not more than six years) to read a sentence. Opening the book at random, she began in a clear distinct voice, "If we do what is right and pleasing before God, he will bless and keep us and make us happy for ever;" and so she went on for a whole page without committing a single mistake in her pronunciation. An expression of parental joy and pride seemed to light up the face of the good Rajah, as he remarked to me at the conclusion, "I believe it is very seldom Hindoo females are ever educated in any other parts of India."

"Seldom, if ever," I replied; "but among the Parsee females in Bombay, there have lately been several instances. Your daughter will prove a rare and remarkable example, and one which I trust may be imitated far and wide."

"But, after all," said the Rajah, "it will be no use to her when she grows up; our women have so many duties to attend to after they are married."

"I believe," said I, "the same may be said of women in every country. But on that account they should still be educated, whether they have the means or power of following up afterwards what they may have learnt in their childhood or not."

"It is my intention," said His Highness, "to

give her in marriage to my nephew, the heir to the throne, at a suitable age."

And after thus summarily disposing of the ultimate destiny of the young lady, she was sent up again to the nursery to her anxious mother.

Soon after this I took my departure.

August 23rd.—To-day Madhava Rao, the tutor recently appointed to instruct the first prince, heir to the throne, and his younger brother, came to pay me a visit. He is a remarkably intelligent young man, about four-and-twenty. He was educated at the Elphinstone College at Madras, where he appears to have been thoroughly grounded both in science and literature, in both of which subjects he is certainly conversant. He was with me for nearly two hours. He spoke English perfectly. His selection of words and phrases was admirable, and he talked with such ease and fluency that I could have given him credit for having been brought up in England, so natural was the language to him. We talked of the American War, of the Reformation, of the discovery of printing, and of English literature in general.

His acquirements were most creditable, to which I have scarcely done justice.*

* The above was written some years ago. Since then Sir T. Madhava Rao, K.S.I., has won for himself the most honourable distinctions, having been successively Dewan at the Courts of Travancore, Indore, and Baroda, from which arduous duties he has at length retired full of honours. He is *par excellence* the most eminent of Indian statesmen. I trust I may with pardonable vanity insert here a letter I received from him in reply to one of mine congratulating him on earning the fruit of his deserved honours.

27th June, 1866.

MY DEAR SIR,—

I am much obliged to you for your very kind note of yesterday, congratulating me on the prospect of my admission to the honour of the Order of the Star of India.

I certainly feel greatly encouraged, the honour being quite unexpected. When I look back upon my career of seventeen years in Travancore, I have abundant cause to thank Heaven for the great happiness vouchsafed to me. The very first source of encouragement was your own favourable report to the late Resident on the result of my labours as tutor to the young princes. It may be in your recollection that you were appointed to examine the princes and to ascertain the progress made by them, and that you went through this task, and made a very favourable report on the results. Ever since that time my position and opportunities have been improving, and my

August 25th.—This morning I donned my blue frock and sash, and ordering my palanquin went to pay the Dewan, Khristno Rao, a visit at his house in the fort. I found him sitting on his bed writing at a small table in front of him. He was partly dressed in a flannel jacket, a flannel skull cap, and pair of loose pyjamas. After a short interval he asked me if I would like to see his child, to which I replied in the affirmative, and a naked boy was brought in.

"This is not my own child," said the Dewan. "It is my adopted son. The fact is, that though I have been married these twenty years, it has not pleased God to bless me with a family. Now, you will remember, sir, about six months ago I was nearly drowned through the upsetting of a boat in the surf. I have often thought since

destiny has now culminated in the attainment of a high honour from Her Majesty's Government.

Again thanking you warmly for your kind congratulations,

I am,

My dear sir,

Yours very sincerely,

T. Madava Rao.

Col. H. Drury,

&c., &c., &c.

then 'Who is there to bear my name if I should die, or be killed suddenly, and left no offspring?' So I looked about among my friends and began to make inquiries, and I discovered my nephew had two sons, so I said to my nephew, 'Give me one of your sons, for I have none.' So after a little time the nephew consented to the transfer, but he would not give up the elder one, but if I chose I might have the youngest. I readily agreed, and took the one he gave me, and this is the one you see now. It does not care for its father or mother now, and loves me more than any one else."

CHAPTER V.

Stories of Tigers—Hill Expeditions—Rajah weighed in Gold—New Year's Day—Balghatty—Singing Birds—Installation of the Rajah of Cochin—Sad Death of a Missionary—Free School at Trevandrum.

OCTOBER 14th.—We have just returned from an expedition to the neighbouring hills, which would have been a more agreeable one if we had not been drenched with rain. We spent the first fifteen days on the Vailey Mullay, where I amused myself laying out a garden for flowers and vegetables, and erecting a temporary hut to keep out the winds which blow here with extraordinary violence during the greater part of the year. The thermometer ranges from 63 to 75 degrees Fahrenheit, and as the bungalow is not more than 2,000 feet above the sea the cold is quite out of proportion to the level. I erected flagstaffs on two of the neighbouring peaks, a hundred feet higher than our station.

From hence I enjoyed a most extensive view of the Travancore Mountains to the north, and the sea and low country to the south and west. We descended again by another ghaut, which in wild scenery was far superior to that on the western side. Large rocky precipices, dense forests, and mountain torrents, at present much swollen by the rains, combined to give this pass a grandeur of character I had not expected to find on this range. At one part I came to I fancied a great resemblance to that gorge in the Tyrolese Alps which opens out upon the romantically situated town of Botzen. The length of this pass was about four miles. Our tents were pitched at the foot in a shady grove of tamarind trees. There was no village, but a Mahommedan Ryot had a farm there, and was the possesser of a few paddy fields. On inquiring of the native superintendent what kind of place we had come to, he replied in his usual quaint way, "This is the tigers' house; all tigers live here; here tigers, there tigers, everywhere tigers." The old man was perfectly correct in his estimate. The locality was infested by them. Among other stories which I heard of their eccentric doings in this neighbourhood, the following was assured as true, though it may be received with a smile of incredulity. Although I will not vouch for the truth, yet I am not inclined to disbelieve the tale altogether. One night a tiger got into a cattle shed and killed seventeen buffaloes out of the herd. After completing the work of destruction, he found the wall from which he had descended too high for him to escape by. So he piled one dead buffalo on to the top of another until he had raised them to a sufficient height for him to use the heaped-up carcasses as a stepping-stone for the purpose of scaling the wall, and in the morning all the dead buffaloes were thus discovered piled in a mass. The second story I was told here was that the villagers one night after hearing a fearful noise of roaring in the jungles went to the place next morning and found a wild hog dead and covered with blood, and only a few yards distant from the boar was a royal tiger also quite dead, gored and covered with wounds. The conflict must have been a fierce one, when both these savage combatants were left dead upon the field. From all I know by experience of the ferocious nature of both these animals I do not doubt for one moment the truth of this tale. Well, we slept safely that night in the "tigers' house," and the next day went across the valley to the opposite range of hills, a distance of about six miles. Our halting place was an elevated plateau about 800 feet from the base of the mountains. Here a missionary has built a small bungalow, in the rear of which is a beautiful cascade, a fall of about sixty feet, though the actual volume of water is not very great. About midway down are two basins, which, by a little artificial assistance, have been converted into excellent bathing pools. We halted here a whole day, and then commenced an ascent to the higher parts of the mountain. In vain we hoped the sun would come out to cheer us on our upward journey, for considering the large amount of wet weather we had experienced lately it was reasonable to suppose that we might look for a favourable change. But the higher we ascended the more persevering was the rain, and worse than all, we got among the clouds, which came rolling over the mountain tops accompanied with frequent and violent gusts of wind. The whole route was excessively steep, which the rains had rendered more difficult, for it had become so slippery that it required the greatest caution and exertion to keep your footing at all, while for every two steps forward you slipped one back, so at this pace of a snail's gallop it was long before we reached our destination. About two-thirds of the way I overtook our baggage elephants with the tent, and found the Mahouts were cutting down a large tree which obstructed the passage.

They cried out to me as I passed, and said the elephant was quite exhausted, and could proceed no farther, and that I must order coolies to be sent to carry the tents. I thought at first that this might be a lazy excuse in their own behalf, but the poor animal went only a few steps further and fairly fell down. This was a sad lookout, but I was really so fatigued myself that I had a great mind to follow the poor brute's example, but as I was wet through and through I pushed on, and at last reached the camping ground.

A few sheds had been hastily erected, and making for the nearest I found the ghost of a fire, but on the servant's telling me there was another separate shed "for master," I went on and entered shed No. 2. I had no change of clothes, and wet as I was I sat down and drank off two glasses of sherry to keep the cold out. What utter misery! In about an hour I was greatly relieved from my distress by seeing the coolies in the distance labouring painfully up the hill with my luggage. In another half-hour I had partly forgotten my griefs, and was soon comfortably wrapped in blankets sitting in an armchair (the rain dropping through the roof however) and reading home letters from Asherton Cottage, which a faithful postman had brought me even to this wild spot of earth. In course of time the tent had come up and was pitched. The squalls, however, continued more and more violent, and it was questionable whether the tent, would stand its ground. It was a small mountain tent, which the Resident and myself just managed to squeeze ourselves into. There was just room for our two cots and half a table; so when dinner was ready, we were obliged to keep the poor servants outside in the cold, for we could spare neither room nor light. Glad was I when we crept into our damp beds, and though I fully anticipated the wreck of our tent by the violent winds, I managed to sleep through the night fairly well.

Scarcely had daylight appeared before we made instant preparations to quit this "inhospitalem Caucasum," and in all our camp there was not one who did not rejoice in our descent to the low country. We proceeded by slow stages till we again reached Trevandrum on the evening of the 25th, neither sick nor sorry.

November 29th.—To Covalom, a marine villa on a cliff about six miles from the capital. This charming spot overlooks the sea from a height of about 150 feet. The view is varied, lovely and extensive. The fresh sea air renders it a most desirable place to sojourn in for a few days, especially during the hot weather. Ships are constantly passing by, which makes the scene very lively and interesting. Next day after arrival I went out with gun and dogs and returned in an hour or so with a hare and brace of jungle-fowl. Game is very plentiful here, especially the latter fowl, a bird no less celeqrated for the beauty of its plumage, than for its delicious flavour when brought to table. A large hyæna rushed out of a bush in front of me and trotted leisurely away, but before I could get my rifle ready he was beyond my reach and speedily disappeared. The natives call the hyæna the tiger-donkey, and from its colour and shape it certainly partakes of the mixed character of both those animals.

December 4th.—We sent tents out three miles to the banks of the Vellarney Lake, a considerable sheet of water, about four miles in length and more than half a mile in breadth. Surrounded as it is by wooded eminences on either side, it has a very pleasing and picturesque appearance. I ascended several summits to gain a survey of the surrounding country, and a noble panorama lay before me. The undulating forest-clad hills stretched far away until arrested by the vast mountain barrier of the Western Ghauts, running from north to south, the extreme limit of the Travancore country.

One morning I embarked on a small canoe, accompanied by a couple of natives, who used the thick stem of a cocoa-palm frond for an oar, and went to the northern end of the lake. At every point the scenery became more varied and lovely. I fired several shots—a difficult proceeding in my frail bark—at large herons and cranes which were plentiful enough on the water, but failed to see any wild duck or teal. As the sun began to wax hot I retraced my steps, and reached the tent about 9 o'clock. My shikarry—native sportsman—asked me if he might go and kill a large crane which he espied stalking about in the shallows. So I let him take the canoe and my gun, and he soon returned triumphant, with a brace of fine large birds, male and female, of a beautiful grey colour mixed with black, the breast being dark brown. The beaks had a red tinge, and they measured about four feet in height. The natives esteem all these kinds of birds as good food, and their eyes glowed at the idea of curried crane, which they had already feasted on in anticipation. But my little servant boy Cassim, a Mussulman, cast a piteous eye upon me as I was distributing the birds to those who had no scruples about what they ate, and he at last spoke out: "I can't eat them, sir, they are dead," and appealing to my shikarry, he said, "Durmiah, go and bring one in half dead, that I may sacrifice and eat it."

But Durmiah did not feel inclined to undertake a second expedition for the express purpose of gratifying Cassim's wishes and appetite, so the poor lad went away disgusted and sorrowful. Just at that moment a villager brought in a live hare in a wicker basket. I immediately cried out "Cassim! Cassim! Here's a live animal, go and pronounce the 'Bismillah,' kill and eat it, all for yourself."

Cassim's face brightened up as he took the hare, and looked as happy as if I had given him a thousand rupees. I should say he came off the best after all.

December 6th.—Struck the tent at daybreak, and getting it packed on the elephant, and the said elephant packing up his own trunk at the same time, and twenty coolies carrying my baggage, I set off across country for the village of Vaulrampoor, a distance of about five miles. My route lay through low jungles, and I arrived about 8 o'clock. While sitting down in the bungalow superintending the unpacking of my traps, I observed a lot of men and boys hunting after something in the street, as if some domestic pet had escaped and they were giving chase. From the position I was in I could not make out what it was, but I saw the people dodging about in all directions, bellowing out, and the crowd increasing in number and adding to the sport. What could be the matter? Several heads popped over the wall to watch the fun, and the little boys in the village seemed to enjoy the "lark" which now appeared at its height. "What is the matter," I asked, as I would not be kept any longer in suspense. "Only catch 'em fowl for master's breakfast," was the reply. I know not if I may attribute it to the previous fright of the chase it had undergone, but it turned out a remarkably fine and tender bird.

December 8th.—How vexed I was with a coolie who had brought me three miles out of the direct road, when there was a shorter path to the tents which I could have run over in half an hour. Late as I was I ascended a hill behind the encamping ground, and asked my guide if I could descend to the other side. "No, sir, too much jungle."

"Is that all?" I asked. "Have you got a knife?"

"Yes, sir."

"Then where there's a will there's a way. Forward!"

"But it's so thick. You cannot get through, and besides the wild animals——"

"On, I say, and not a word. You see that large tree yonder. Make straight for that. Go we must."

So the guide finding remonstrance in vain pushed forward to pioneer as best he could, while I followed with a large clasp knife, cutting and clearing away the branches as well as I was able.

"Oh! sir, the thorns," every now and then cried out the coolie. But it was no use thinking of thorns then, and I encouraged him to proceed as it was no use to turn back. When we reached the thickest part of that dark and gloomy jungle I stopped, and addressing my guide, said, "Now, listen to me. A demon lives here, and as sure as possible, if you don't take care, you'll meet him, and so I advise you to get out of the wood as quick as may be." The poor fellow did not know which way to turn, nor could I assist him, for we had lost all sight of the open sky, and were hemmed in by a dense thicket. However, we persevered, and eventually emerged into the open, the guide being agreeably surprised to find himself safe once more. But I took the opportunity to read him a lesson, and said,

"Never again tell an Englishman there is no road to this or that place. Do you understand?"

"I understand, sir," he feebly answered and walked away.

Thursday.—After a few days' rest I am again on the move, and leaving in my palanquin about 4 A.M., ran out half-way to Neddavancaud, a village in the forests, about twelve miles off. At daybreak I quitted the palanquin and rode the remaining part of the journey. The air was bracing and cold, and a heavy dew overspread the green fields of Paddy, looking as if a shower of pearls had fallen on beds of emerald. On reaching the tents I made immediate arrangements for a battue in the forests, which in all conscience were thick enough here, and for that purpose summoned to attendance all the native sportsmen I could collect together. They came in dozens, all armed with guns and matchlocks, a mighty preparation indeed, as if we were bent upon exterminating every wild animal from the face of the country. About eleven o'clock I mounted my little pony and rode upwards of three miles into the interior until I came to a very neat farm-house partly surrounded by rice-fields, partly by jungle. I went inside to seek shelter from the sun, while the natives held a council of war regarding the sport. I was so charmed with this dwelling, and it was so retired, and so lovely, in its situation, that I resolved to remain here two or three days, and so sent for all my baggage and servants to be brought here at once. The proprietor of the farm allotted me his granary, added to which was a small verandah. Here I had a table placed where I took my meals, while I managed to stow away my cot inside, there being just enough room for it, the floor being strewed with herbs, fruits and seeds.

Everything was comfortably arranged. Oh! this wild kind of life! How I loved it! One day I went a distance of four or five miles further in these backwoods, where I thought habitations of man and man himself must cease; but here also I found a pleasant dwelling, shaded by palms and large forest trees, and the whole surroundings wearing an air of cleanly comfort and ease so often found amid the peasants' houses in Travancore. This latter place was far more romantically situated. The hills which enclosed the charming little valley were loftier, and here I came upon the recent tracks of elephants and deer which had been running riot only the previous night over the rice plantations. I could have sojourned many more days amid the calm retirement of these peaceful scenes and happy people, but the serious illness of a friend summoned me from the joyous contemplation of these glorious scenes of nature, to the melancholy duty of attending a deathbed.

May 9th.—A ceremony peculiar, I fancy, to Travancore, is about to come off at the palace. The Rajah is to be weighed in gold. This is his real coronation, and constitutes him half a Brahmin. When he has passed through the golden cow, he becomes a full Brahmin, and much good may it do him. On occasion of the first ceremony the other day, about two lakhs of rupees were spent altogether, and this taken from the cash-chest of a bankrupt state. The Rajah's weight was one and a half lakhs, the remaining half lakh was spent in preparations and gifts. In fact the whole was given away in food and coin to the Brahmins only, a reprehensible custom, where in an impoverished state as Travancore now is, the enormous sum of £20,000 is wrung forcibly from the poor to be given to the rich. The salaries of nearly all the lower class of public servants are now five or six months in arrear, the result of this forced demand for money for this shameful and abhorred custom. And the Brahmins go back to their homes filled with food and laden with money to add to their already overflowing heaps, while the poor of other castes are absolutely starving from their small pittance being now denied them. The two ceremonies take place once during the lifetime and reign of each successive Rajah. It is, of course, a source of immense profit to the Brahmins, and the more Rajahs, the more gain. The last Rajah died in 1846. He drooped and succumbed a few months after the second ceremony, in the flower of his age. No one dared to whisper the cause of his sudden decease, but some few guessed, and perhaps rightly. So there came another Rajah, and another golden cow.

January 1st.—What a distracting, tiresome day this first of January is in India, owing to the complimentary visits, very well intentioned, of every native official, high and low. From the Dewan down to the grass cutter every man brings in his goodwill-offering in the shape of a lime, a bunch of plantains, oranges, raisins and sugar, till the tables groan with the weight of fruit, and a relay of trays can scarcely convey them all away to the store-room. Shaddocks, too, and pomegranates may be enumerated among the gifts, and garlands of flowers besides. It is a mark of respect from an inferior to approach one of higher caste with a lime, accompanied by a profound salaam. Among

Rajahs, Governors, and all *haute noblesse* the offerings are Cashmere shawls, and bags of gold mohurs, but the principle is the same.

12th.—My Shikarry brought in this morning two hyænas he had killed about seven miles from this. He shot them at night while sitting up for wild hog. In default of the latter animal making its appearance he slew the first named brutes—first come first served.

15th.—A great hubbub at the palace owing to the abstraction of a celebrated idol from the Pagoda at Allepey. The iconoclepts have borne it off rather triumphantly into the Cochin territory, from whence it originally came many years ago. In former years it would have been made a *casus belli* between the two states. Great bribes were given for the successful accomplishment of the rape, and no doubt the highest officials in the Cochin territory were promoters of the theft. The Rajah is mad with vexation. It appears that a great deal of veneration has ever been attached to this idol, which is a diminutive figure of the god Khrishna, about eight inches in height and cut out of a kind of greenstone, and called emerald. It is known as the Bimbum. A mysterious virtue has always been attached to this little god in granite, for prosperity is always said to follow in his wake, and where he is not there will be adversity. Travancore has lost her tutelary deity, and confusion awaits the kingdom consequently. The Rajah is furious against his minister and expels him from his presence. The minister, in tears, comes up to the Resident and remains with him till late at night, and threatens to leave the country, he feels in such disgrace. Alas! for the superstitious follies of mankind. The Rajah is at his wits' end, and has abandoned all hopes of future happiness and glory because half-a-dozen crafty Brahmins have removed a piece of stone from one temple to another. Poor Travancore! Thy glory has departed. The Medes and Persians are coming.

18th.—The papers announce the establishment of a native police for Madras and the outlying districts, under the superintendence of Mr. Robinson, the Police Magistrate. I should not think it worth while to mention this circumstance were it not for the following *jeu d'esprit* to which it gave rise, which has a humorous ring about it.

THE MODEL POLICEMAN OF MADRAS.

For twenty long years
  A Perlisseman I have been,
And such a go as this
  I'm blessed, I've never seen.

It seems a Hinjian beak
  Is raisin of a force
To keep the prigs away
  According to the lors.

A Peeler there must be,
  As strong as any hox,
As hactive as a squirrel,
  As cunning as a fox.

He must be firm and just,
  Likewise highly truthful,
Never take his lush,
  Not a single toothful.

Discretion he must have
  Temper too, and tact,
Down on all their dodges,
  Up to every knack.

Never riled himself,
  Never riling others,
Looking on the blacks
  Just as little brothers.

Zeal and eddication
  Up to any figger,
Must that Peeler have
  Who'd catch a prigging Nigger.

Diligent and hactive
  Must this Peeler be,
Business-like in abits
  Regular to a T.

A little tin in 'and
  Ighly indispensable,
Howing of a bob
  Being indefensible.

He must do his work
  In a liberal spirit,
Getting lots to do,
  Precious little for it.

'Osses he must keep
  In number two at least,
No ass can do the work,
  Nor other sort of beast.

Fermiliar must he be
  With their way of talking,
Learning of their lingo,
  On his beat a-walking.

Learned in the law
  Must the Bobby be,
Who'd serve the Hinjian beak
  In that capacity.

Oh ! Mr. Robinson,
  Listen to the lay
Of a poor London Peeler,
  Vich his name's Perlisseman A.

When you've tried in vain
  Your perlisse ranks to fill
(Men cannot be your Peelers,
  And Hangels never will),

Just write a line to me
  To say you want a man,
Who's active, firm and upright,
  And who'll do the best he can.

You may drop the other qualities,
  The three I've named will do ;
Address to Perlisseman A,
  Vich his number's forty-two.

8th.—*Balghatty.* Any one coming here will remark a quantity of blue limestone arranged in patches all over the grass, and will wonder what they are and where they come from. The Resident's passion for geology is the only solution of this question. This allusion to scientific pursuits puts me in mind of a story of a waggish trick having been played upon the Governor of Woolwich one fine day, when he presided at a lecture on mineralogy and geology given for the edification of the cadets. The latter were seated at either side of a long table, and the Governor and lecturer together at the top of the same. Each specimen was first labelled, then shown to the Governor, and then passed round among the cadets. Among these was one youngster who, more inclined to wit than science, happened to see under that part of the table he was near to a large fungus growing. In an instant he conceives the idea of passing off a joke upon the meeting. Whipping a knife out of his pocket he cuts a large slice out of the fungus, dark on the upper side and pale below, and, shaping it a little, he labelled it with a piece of paper as "The tongue of a Prussian Cat," and passed it round. Everyone appeared astonished at this marvellous specimen of feline anatomy, till at last, like all other specimens, it came in its turn to the Governor and lecturer. Now the former individual was rather deaf, and the specimen being handed in, both he and those around him were exceedingly perplexed as to the nature of this wonderful tongue. The Governor was angry that it had not at first been shown to him.

The lecturer, again, could not explain how it had escaped his observation, and the Governor said: "What kind of cats have they in Prussia? Have you ever seen one alive? Have you the skin of one? They must be very extraordinary cats." At last the lecturer, guessing what had been done, said: "It is all a joke, sir—a harmless bit of wit—very innocent, Colonel."

"Eh? eh?" said the Governor, getting more deaf as his ideas became confused on the subject of the cat. "Eh? what? the animal is harmless—quite innocent? What a peculiar kind of cat! What colour are these Prussian cats?" Every one by this time was in roars of laughter, till at last the Governor was brought to comprehend the joke that had been played off upon him. When rising, with a voice of thunder, he called out "Silence!" and it ended in the cadets being all marched home and the meeting dispersed.

11th.—The H.C. steamer *Semiramis* called to-day at the port (Cochin) on her way from Rangoon to Bombay, and one of the young officers was sent over here to ask if the Resident had any treasure to remit by her. During the visit the young middy said, by way of opening conversation: "Have you been long in this country, sir?" "Not very," was the reply; "about half a century." The poor boy nearly fainted away; but imagined it was a joke, and told me afterwards that he was not so green as to be taken in in that way. It was, nevertheless, quite true. Talking of officers of long standing in the service, I mentioned at dinner the story of General Whitelock, who, when in command at Portsmouth, in 1804, was in the habit of going out in disguise at night, and on one unlucky occasion was caught by a press gang of sailors and taken on board their ship for enlistment, the mistake not being discovered until next morning. The Resident told a further anecdote about the same officer. He was appointed to the command of the ill-fated expedition to Buenos Ayres, at the beginning of the century, and, together with other distinguished officers, was taken prisoner. When the British Government solicited an interchange of prisoners, in connection with certain arrangements of peace, they specially demanded the release of General Whitelock, "trusting that the Spanish Government would respect the grey hairs of age." To this a reply was sent "that the Spanish Government recognized no plea for sparing grey hairs, but always entertained a respect for *white locks*, and therefore consented to his release."

23rd.—This morning a native lad named Mootookistnah, who paints flowers, collects specimens, and executes various little offices for the Resident, came to me and asked how long it was likely the Resident would remain away from Trevandrum, "because," he said, "my poor mother is crying very much, and has not ate her food for several days, and this is the first time we have been separated, and she will be very unhappy till I get back again." "Ah, Mootoo," I replied, "you are not the only one, recollect, who has to lament being absent from those dear to them. It is the first time of leaving your mother, but you must try and accustom yourself to these temporary absences. I don't think you are likely to see your mother for the next four months, for the Resident has no intention of returning to Trevandrum for a long time, and what will you do then?" "In that case I should resign my situation with the Resident; my mother would make me do so." "Nonsense, Mootoo; bear it like a man. Why I have not seen my mother for eight years, and, perhaps, may not see her again in this world." "Ah, sir, that is what we natives cannot understand. You English not only leave your parents to come out to this country, but you do more; you send away your wives and children from this country to England. We couldn't do that, sir." I had no time to explain to him the expediency and necessity of banishing our families from us for a time, but bade him write and tell his mother that she would see him again sooner than she expected. With this the boy seemed satisfied, and went away.

28th.—It's an erroneous notion, and yet a very common one, that there are no singing birds in India. Alison in his History asserts that "the forests are not enlivened with the notes of the songster." If any one trusts such a mistaken statement regarding the silence of the feathered tribe in the tropics, and had been with me at Allwaye last week, he would have been disillusioned from that false idea for ever. The birds sing there exquisitely; not much in the daytime, perhaps, but chiefly at break of dawn and an hour after sunrise. I have listened while in bed, charmed with their melodies; these, not so much from a single bird sitting on a bough, like our thrush and robin, but the groves resound with the united harmony of numberless birds, with nothing harsh or discordant in their symphonies. As an individual songster I have never heard the notes of the Wagtail equalled. I never heard this bird sing in England—possibly it does, but here its note is most sweet. And there is a black and white bird, about the size of a robin, and with the same habits, whose notes are also very sweet. Some birds sing at night —chiefly on moonlight nights. There is something so soothing and calm at night time in the tropics, when the moon is shining brightly, that the very birds seem loth to take their natural repose, singing as for joy throughout the midnight hours. There is one particular bird which, during the months of April and

May, may be heard every night in the forests on the coasts, and probably elsewhere. It is a migratory bird, and night and day you may hear the "Sota tha." There is a tradition connected with this bird, which relates that when Adam, according to the Creator's instructions, had summoned all the birds on a stated day to be present in the garden of Paradise that he might name them, this bird, of all the rest was late, and on Adam inquiring the reason of his not being in time, he replied "Mein sota tha" (or "I was sleeping"). "Then," said Adam, "that shall be your name, and from this time you shall never sleep again." The peculiar note this bird utters is precisely as any one would pronounce in two lines, or pauses,—

Mĕin sŏ
tŭ thā.

And so the curse rests upon this poor bird, and through the longest, darkest nights often have I heard this plaintive, melancholy wail, when not a breath of wind, nor hum of insect, nor any other noise is heard besides.

6th.—Yesterday was the installation of the

new Rajah. We assembled at the Palace at 11 A.M. There were about a dozen Europeans. The natives of course mustered in force, and the troops consisted of about 100 rank and file. The Rajah received the Resident in the Durbar room upstairs, and conducting him to a chair, sat himself down on the Resident's left hand, the Europeans taking seats down the room, right and left. After some preliminary small talk, the Resident proposed to lift His Highness on the throne, and beckoned to me to assist in the ceremony. But such was the awkwardness of the Rajah that he would not turn properly round for the purpose, and as he could not speak English, there was no possibility of making him understand, so he fiddled about with his arms and hands till the people must have wondered what the Resident and I were doing to him. At last the former, getting out of all patience, catches hold of his right arm and gives him a twist right round, and then we both seized him and forcibly planted him on the musnud, and so all happily, and I trust respectfully, ended. Then was read the proclamation inside and outside the Hall, but the troops outside instead of firing a *feu-de-joie* fired a funeral volley, a most ominous mistake, and were the natives to learn the error that had been committed, their superstitious fears would certainly lead them to believe that His Highness must come to an untimely end. At the last Installation the Resident forgot to bring the Proclamation, and to that circumstance alone they attributed the early decease of the last Prince. Well! I have just assisted to place a King on a throne. Strange indeed if my next duty was to help to *de*throne one, as I have just received intimation that my services will be required to join the expeditionary army to Burmah.

10th.—Just before dinner the Resident sends me down a note saying, "Look at the shoals of fish. What a time for the fishermen!" In an instant I let down the large fishing net which is opposite my bungalow, and in less than five minutes succeeded in securing a most miraculous draught of fishes. A shoal had passed over the net. I never witnessed such a sight. The difficulty was to get them out. After baling them out with a hand-net by hundreds, very little progress was made in diminishing the numbers after twenty minutes work. So we got a boat about fifteen feet long, and a large wicker basket, and threw them out in enormous quantities. A person standing in the boat was ankle-deep in fish. The canoe from one end to the other was filled, and the fish were six inches deep. I cannot be beyond the mark when I say there must have been from 15,0co to 18,000 fish caught in that one haul. Every servant in the establishment had a large basketful given him, and there are not a few servants at the Residency. The Resident's bearers had alone ten large baskets full. They were a small kind of fish, like sardines, about six or eight inches long.

20th.—I was on the point of embarking at ten o'clock last night for the purpose of going to Quilon, when a sudden squall came on, and it blew and rained furiously. The lightning and thunder were terrific, and the waves dashed against the stone facing near my bungalow, such as I had never witnessed before. All of a sudden my servant rushes into my room to announce a wreck. I at once ordered a Residency boat to be manned and brought round to try and save the unfortunates in this dreadful storm. In less than ten minutes the rescue boat came round opposite my house, which was close upon the water, and strove to launch out in the wind's teeth, while all the light was by the momentary flashes of lightning. We kept lanterns on shore to direct the boat if possible, and by way of encouraging the poor fellows whose cries for assistance we heard through the gloom. In a few minutes we lost the tract of our boat in the surrounding darkness. It was a time of anxious suspense to us on shore, but after a short interval she came back having saved three lives from inevitable drowning. They, poor men, had been capsized in their canoe, and were struggling against the waves when my boat came up with them and opportunely rescued them from a watery grave. Our boatmen were handsomely rewarded, and I ordered these poor half-drowned fellows to be given another boat in which they might proceed to their own homes after the storm had ceased.

26th.—*Camp at Oodagherry.* Heard a good story to-day which I must record here. On the occasion of the arrival at Madras of the recently appointed Governor, most of the influential and respectable merchants and tradesmen went to Government House to pay their customary respects. Among the latter was a Mr. Pharaoh, who has long been the head of a most enterprising and well-known firm in the publishing line. The Governor, who of course feels it incumbent on him to ask some question, or to make some civil remark to all who come to pay their respects on this first occasion, said to Mr. Pharaoh, "Have you ever been to England?"

"I think, your Excellency, I may say that I have been up and down the Red Sea about fourteen times in my life."

"Indeed," remarked the Governor. "Well! you are certainly more fortunate than your ancestor. He tried it only once, and got drowned for his pains."

28th.—To Oodagherry. The wind here was very violent. It is interesting to watch the heavy masses of clouds seeking the mountains during this season of the monsoon, though so far south as we are they considerably lessen in size, and the fall of rain is much diminished. Eight miles beyond this, and we are out of the influence of the monsoon altogether. The mountains break up into smaller masses, and become more jagged and uneven in their summits, and certainly less clothed with vegetation, easily accounted for by the less amount of moisture they receive. I have often remarked a peculiar sight at this season when staying at Nagercoil. A line of clouds, when arrested by a range of mountains, attains and remains at a certain elevation. Beyond Nagercoil there is a low pass in the mountains, eight or ten miles wide, with lofty hills on either side. This uniform line of cloud stretches from one side of the pass to the other without its being broken, and consequently the observer can see beneath it and beyond it, and while on this side all is cloud and rain in a gloomy atmosphere, one can see beyond, the cheerful sunshine and burning plains of the Carnatic, where not a cloud is to be seen. The extreme contrast between the two climates which are here brought into one view has more than once led my mind to imagine fancifully the likeness of this bleak and dark world, and the bright and cheerful one beyond. Winds and storms go dashing with fruitless violence against yon mountain barrier, but there they end. They cannot pass further. There is a glimpse of light beyond where the sun is ever shining, and that pass in the mountains is the "narrow way" that leads to it, and they who enter into that sunny region leave behind them the storms that have so long agitated and encompassed them here.

Rode over this morning to a missionary station to investigate a complaint. The villagers have so encroached upon all the roads in the neighbourhood of the mission that the house was completely "hedged in," to use the most expressive term, and consequently difficult of approach from any quarter. How very comfortably these reverend brethren of L. M. S. live. Their dwelling-houses are excellent ones, well-furnished, and of capital size. I remained here the whole day, and directed two roads to be opened first, and afterwards a third one, which I trust will satisfy the complainants. The name of this station was originally Peyoor or Devil-town, but this would never do, grating harshly upon the ears of a gospel-preacher, so it was re-baptized Sandapooram, or the Village of Peace. The next morning after breakfast walked to a deserted fort called Wuttacotta about two miles off from another missionary station known as Jamestown, quite in the wilderness. The fort is still in good condition as far as solidity goes, but it cannot be more than eighty years old, erected at the same time as the lines to keep out the inroads of Tippoo, and the numerous marauders who formerly infested the Tinnevelly district. It is on the shore, and one wing is carried out some thirty yardsinto the sea, to prevent any invaders getting round by the coast road. The labour expended on the construction of this petty fortress must have been very great, and the amount of misery entailed upon the people by forced labour of the kind is fearful to contemplate.

November 19th.—On the Vailey Mullay hill, 2,000 feet. While sitting outside my hut this morning taking a cup of tea I descried a herd of bison grazing in the valley below. Called the Resident to look at them. "Oh! how grand," he exclaimed. Got my gun and sallied after them. A long tramp through the high grass wet with dew. I got two shots, but never expected to kill with the small ordnance I had with me. The beasts walked off very leisurely, but they ascended hills too steep for me to follow them up.

August 17th.—*Trevandrum.* Mr. Leitch, a medical Missionary was accidentally drowned yesterday while bathing at Mootum, a place about thirty miles down the coast. A year ago I was collecting subscriptions for him to build a hospital for the Mission at Neyoor, and, moreover, furnished him with a plan of a building for the purpose, as I was then in temporary charge of the engineer's office. He was very grateful for the little assistance I could give him, and I was to have gone and seen it now it was completed. But it was not to be. In a moment he was gone. He sank at once, and no doubt exists in my mind but that he was seized by a shark. The other Missionary who was bathing with him had reached the shore, and looking back saw nothing of his friend, nor was his body ever found. Thus was a career of great usefulness and promise at once extinguished by one of those mysterious ways of Providence so incomprehensible to us. By his exertions and indefatigable labour he relieved the wants and necessities of hundreds, nay thousands, of the sick poor, sick both in body and soul. And only one year had he laboured in his ministry when he was summoned to meet his reward.

Wednesday 18th.—Went with the Resident to an examination at the Free School. The Rajah and suite, Prime Minister, and all officials were present. The students answered very fairly. About three classes were examined. The recitations of poetry were very good. It did seem strange to see a Christian and a Brahmin standing side by side in the same class reciting the "Crucifixion," each taking alternate verses, or rather stanzas. The Bible is here a text-book; nor has any objection been taken to its introduction. Instruction given to the lads in this school is in every way praiseworthy and well carried out. The purity of the English spoken by natives in Travancore has often been remarked upon, and the language has been disseminated through all classes in the country. I remember travelling in my palanquin at night in the Salem district. My bearers lost their way in an uninhabited part of the country, having attempted a short cut. I was prepared to pass the night where I was, till suddenly a native approached my palanquin and addressed me in English. I was so astonished that I asked him where he came from. "From Travancore," he replied, "a scholar of the Free School." He spoke to the bearers, pointed out the right road, and running by the side of my Palkee did not quit me till all was safe. So when at this school I heard Brahmins and all other castes being examined in the "Reformation," "Book of Proverbs," and other subjects, I could easily foresee the sure but silent stroke which would gradually but certainly undermine the errors of Heathenism.

CHAPTER VI.

Slavery—Improvements in the Country—Letter from Madava Rao—Botany—Commercial Products—Conclusion.

MY connection with Travancore was now drawing to a close, and it was with feelings of sincere regret that I turned my back upon a country where I had spent so many happy years of my life. With the reigning Rajah I always had the most friendly intercourse. He is the personification of good nature, and were he not so blindly submissive to the evil counsels of native advisers he would have grand opportunities of promoting to a greater extent the welfare of his subjects. But Brahminism prevails and probably there is no help for it. "As my kingdom was in my predecessors' time, so let it remain, and so let it descend to my heir." I fear this sentiment—this doctrine—is too strongly implanted in royal breasts to be argued or combatted by opposite counsels. Now, as a case in point, the Resident has been for some time taking measures for abolishing slavery in Travancore, and with this view he pointed out to the Rajah, among other forcible arguments, the esteem he would be held in not only by his neighbouring states, but even in Europe and other parts of the world. "True," argued the prince, "but the landed proprietors do not wish it, and I could never do anything that was not agreeable to all my subjects. "But," replied the Resident, "they will incur no loss. My desire is to free the next generation, and to emancipate children yet unborn; an act which I am sure your Highness will approve of. It is hardly fair that any child before it can distinguish right from wrong, should be born and live in slavery, without a choice."

"Most assuredly," rejoined the prince, "and as far as I am concerned, I should wish to abolish the practice at once. But it has never been done before, and I should not like to make any alteration myself in the existing state of affairs."

The everlasting *but* did not eventually prevail, and after a little pressure from the higher authorities, the blot of slavery has been wiped out from the land.

It was about the same time that a delicate question was mooted among the Missionaries regarding the adoption of a more suitable adornment for those native women who had become converts in their schools. That some enforced regulation should be made had long been obvious to all who had any respect for common decency, and the lax observation of any established rule upon the mode of dress, or rather undress, upon the upper parts of their person was notorious to all who had ever visited the country. The Missionaries were the first, and properly so, to raise an outcry against the scandalous deficiency in question; but they met with the most determined opposition from the higher castes, and notably the Brahmins, who resisted by all the influence they possessed any innovation in this particular. The matter at one time became very serious, and seemed likely to terminate in more or less rioting in the districts. The palace authorities and the

Brahmins were of course at one upon the issue, and the British Resident could but give advice upon the subject. The "Upper Cloth" question, as it was called, was everywhere discussed and commented on. I happened to be at Madras for a short interval about this time, and during an interview with H. E. the Governor he alluded among other things to the cloth question, and said, "You have just come from Travancore, I believe?" I replied in the affirmative. "You are of course aware," he continued, "that communications have lately been going on between the two Governments about female converts being required to wear the upper cloth." I said I knew that discussions had taken place upon the question, and that great opposition was shown by the higher castes. "Well," he said, "when you return to Trevandrum you may tell the authorities that the affair shall be carried out on behalf of the women, *even at the point of the bayonet.*" Strong words these, I thought. But as the bearer of so important an injunction, I never hesitated in my duty of delivering it. Happily no bayonet was eventually required. The Missionaries gained the day, and with a few unimportant reservations, a compromise was effected, and the result upon the whole was favourable to the female community. At any rate a great step was gained in advance towards a higher sense of morality and civilisation.

The native appellation of the country is Tiruvankodu, meaning the "Land of Charity," and I believe the name to be thus accounted for. It has always been a law in Travancore that a Brahmin shall never die of starvation in that country. With the view of acting up to the letter of this law, certain establishments have been provided in various parts of the land for preserving and distributing rice daily to the poorer classes of Brahmins. The buildings wherein the stores are kept are called Ootoo-perahs, and their management, as unhappily is sometimes the case in charitable institutions, has been subjected to great abuse and mis-direction both of funds as well as of substance. They formed a considerable item of expenditure in the annual accounts, and some years ago when the revenue was sensibly decreasing, and it was necessary to adopt strong measures for ameliorating the financial affairs of the state, these Ootooperahs were found to be a source of needless waste, and it was resolved to put their expenditure upon a more economical footing, for it was notorious that it was not only the poor and deserving who benefit by the daily distribution of these charitable doles, but many persons who never could need relief took advantage of a gratis distribution of rice, so freely and liberally supplied.

During the short period that I was the officiating Resident I took every available opportunity of developing the resources of the country, and effecting such reform and improvement as my short tenure of office would allow of. Happily I had so wise and strenuous a coadjutor as Madava Rao—the famous statesman I have previously spoken of. He was always ready to bring his influence and authority as Prime Minister to bear upon any matter conducive to the interests and welfare of the country. The subjoined extract from one of his letters to me will show how eagerly he grasped at any proposal for the amelioration of the existing state of things, and how clearly his arguments *pro* and *con* were put forth :—

TREVANDRUM,
August 17th.

MY DEAR SIR,—

Your last letter from Quilon has proved very gratifying to me on many accounts.

I quite concur with you in all your observations touching the capabilities of Travancore. It seems to me plain that this country is destined, under certain obvious conditions, to become one of the most opulent and enviable parts of India.

Yes. Travancore ought to enter the lists against Wynaad before long. The whole subject of coffee planting is one of great importance to the country, and hence it may be desirable to pay early attention to it. The progress of the country would not be very rapid unless foreign capital is imported. The task of pushing forward the confines of agricultural production is now chiefly devolved on a few poor Ryots, who find it impossible to do anything on a tolerably large scale ; such natives as have capital apparently prefer to invest it in land long since brought under culture and improved. They hardly possess enterprise enough to be tempted to new undertakings. The example of the achievements of foreign capital and enterprise will probably rouse the energies of the native capitalist also.

The subject has been under my anxious consideration. I hope soon to mature my thoughts on this head. The essential, and indeed the most indispensable, object is of course to grant perfect security. The profits of industry and capital must be most strongly ensured to their owner. Strangely, this all important object seems to have been much lost sight of for a series of years past. A class of land, by no means inconsiderable in extent has, up to this, been subject to a kind of tenure of so much uncertainty, that the tenant was not sure of reaping the next crop! A rule has been brought into operation from the first day of this year by which this class of land is to be hereafter leased out for a period of ten years. This term may answer for that particular class of land. But where the culture of land, now jungle, is concerned, of course the term should be *far* longer.

As you observe, the importance of Allepey as

a port ought to be better known. From the last impression of the *Cochin Courier* I see that subject is drawing attention. A lighthouse is a want at Allepey, which I hope will soon be supplied.

Then again, as to the deepening of the bar at Neendacurray, I do not know if the feasibility of the thing was ever professionally examined into. When we shall have acquired a certain degree of impetus in the public works department, *i.e.*, when we shall find that we shall need an engineer of our own to devote his services and energies to this country, we might then make arrangements accordingly.

I hope you will excuse the length of this letter, though I should say that one's self-control is heavily taxed when he has to resist the temptation of such a subject as the improvement of this fine country.

Yours very faithfully,

T. MADAVA RAO.

An allusion is made in the above letter to the question of a lighthouse being erected at the port of Allepey. Without any ambition to blow my own trumpet, I hope I may quote in this place a paragraph from the journal above quoted touching upon certain contemplated improvements, several of which have been carried out since I left the country. "It is always gratifying to us to chronicle the meritorious acts of public officers, and it is with much pleasure that we notice the efforts made by Major Drury, the Acting Resident, during the brief period he has been in charge of the office, to promote works of public utility, the advantages of which had been felt and acknowledged, but which unhappily had not emerged from the shadowy regions of the imagination into accomplished facts. The projects which we understand Major Drury is about to carry out at once, are of the utmost importance, and will afford extensive facilities for commerce. One of these is the erection of a pier at Allepey 500 feet long and thirty broad —a boon which will no doubt be appreciated by the entire mercantile community, as offering them great conveniences for shipment, and superseding the clumsy contrivances which have hitherto been in use for that purpose.

"A still more valuable improvement is the

erection of a lighthouse to guide the shipping into the safe and convenient port of Allepey, in case of stress of weather. This has been the great desideratum of this excellent port, as certified by several Masters of British vessels in a letter which recently appeared in these columns; and now that it is about to be supplied through the wise foresight of the Acting Resident, it will render the port more easily accessible to ships of all nations as a harbour of refuge. These, however, are not the only acts of Major Drury. Many other things have been brought to our notice, where by supporting the Dewan in carrying out an enlightened policy, he has commenced the good work which we hope now to see spread its happy influence over that magnificent, but long misgoverned country, Travancore."

And was the lighthouse ever built, the reader will ask. Yes—but *tulit alter honores.*

It may readily be supposed that a country like Travancore affords ample field for the researches of the botanist, and this is undoubtedly the case. Frequent as have been the explorers on the western coast, in Canara, Malabar and

Coorg, the highlands of Travancore and Cochin have seldom been visited, and although the larger portion of the Flora partakes of a character resembling that of the neighbouring districts, yet it is not improbable that some plants considered peculiar to Ceylon may be found on these mountains. Whatever may have been the shortcomings of the administration of the Dutch East India Company, it is certain that they had at least the redeeming qualities of not having neglected to promote the study of science, and the development of the natural resources of the countries they settled in. Few subjects are deserving of greater attention than those which derive their value from being connected with the comforts and necessities of human life. And the most attractive of all sciences are those which lead in their results, from every fresh discovery or application of a principle, to a permanent benefit on behalf of mankind. Among such we may look upon botany as taking a high rank, and it is to the lasting praise of the Dutch that their labours in the cause of science in India were so zealous, and which entitle them to be ranked as the earliest pioneers in this field.

Bartolomeo devotes an entire chapter in his work to this subject. "India alone," he says, "contains more medical writings than are to be found in all the rest of the world. As printing has never been introduced here, all hands are employed in copying manuscripts, and particularly such as relate to the prolongation of human life—namely, medical and botanical. Both these sciences were cultivated in India above 3,000 years ago, and at present give employment to a great number of people. When a physician is sent for, you are sure to be visited by five or six. There are even boys who possess an extensive knowledge of botany, and this is not surprising, as from their earliest years they are made acquainted with the nature of plants and their different properties." To these remarks succeed a catalogue of several medicinal plants, with their uses and properties, together with the vernacular names, and which, according to his own account, cost him an immense degree of labour to collect. But he must have been mainly indebted to the industry of his Dutch predecessors, who, a century before his time, had been collecting plants, and illustrating with indefatigable reśearch the flora of this coast.

Foremost in the ranks of these early Dutch botanists stands the name of Henricus Van Rheede, Governor of Cochin, who laid the whole country under contribution for his unequalled work in twelve folio volumes on the plants of the western coast. "The 'Hortus Malabaricus,'" says Evelyn, "presents us with the most stupendous and unheard of plants in that elaborate work, the cuts being in copper, and certainly of any published the most accurate done, nor are they in their shape and description less surprising."* In this famous work are contained 794 plates, so accurately figured that there is no difficulty whatever in identifying them. Next followed Rumphius, a Hanoverian, whose "Herbarium Amboinense" occupies six quarto volumes, with about 780 plates. Hermann, whose labours were confined to Ceylon, and the two Burmanns, father and son, whose "Flora Indica" and "Flora Zeylanica" respectively are valuable repertories of Indian botanical lore. Koenig was a Dane, Commelin, Klein,

* Evelyn Correspondence, 1681.

and Rottler were either Dutch or German. All honour then to the Hollanders who first laid the foundation of that edifice which the subsequent labours of Roxburgh, Wallich, and Wight have wellnigh completed in the present century. Subsequent researches have rendered Bartolomeo's list of plants anything but novel or valuable, though doubtless it cost him considerable labour to collect his numerous specimens and to add their Latin, Malabar, and Portuguese names. "The sources I employed," he says, "besides my own experience, are the dictionaries of Hanxleden, Viscoping, and Pimental, the 'Herbarium' of Father Fraz, and a MS. containing observations by many regular physicians and botanists, natives of the coast of Malabar." Whatever may be the value of the learned treatises above referred to, we fear they are inaccessible to the student of the present day, who must content himself with more recent and withal worthier books on the flora of the western coast. The climate of Travancore is the same as in other parts of Malabar, and the following remarks by the most eminent of modern botanists may be applied to this country :—"From the humid character of the Malabar climate its luxuriant vegetation might be inferred. Hamilton tells us that it resembles Bengal in verdure, but has loftier trees and more palms; the shores are skirted with cocoanuts, and the villages surrounded with groves of betel nut, palms, and talipots. Vateria Indica, a noble dipterocarpous tree, is abundantly planted in many parts; cassia, pepper, and cardamoms flourish wild in the jungles, and form staple products for export. The low valleys are richly clothed with rice fields, and the hill sides with millets and other dry crops, whilst the gorges and slopes of the loftier mountains are covered with a dense and luxuriant forest."* Pepper grows well in the lowlands, but with far more luxuriance in elevated tracks and hilly regions. It is planted in the neighbourhood of trees, as the vine requires support. The plants, which climb to a great height, last generally from eighteen to twenty years, when other grafts or shoots are substituted for them.

* Hooker and Thomson's "Introductory Essay to the Flora of India."

For centuries pepper has been an article of exportation to Europe from these countries, and although growing elsewhere, Malabar pepper is reckoned the best. On an average calculation about 5,000 candies are annually produced in Travancore. It has been erroneously supposed that the white and black pepper are from different plants, but this is not the case. When the corns are dried they acquire a black colour, but if kept some years the outer coating disappears, and the peppercorns appear white.

Another valuable production is the cardamom, which is either cultivated or gathered wild. In the Travancore forests the plant is found at elevations from 3,000 to 5,000 feet. The ground is simply cleared of forest trees, when the plants spontaneously grow up from the cleared patches in the space of about three months. Great quantities are annually shipped to Europe from Malabar and Travancore. In the latter country they are a monopoly. The cultivators come from the British provinces on the other side of the Ghauts.

There are other staple exports of minor value,

such as turmeric, cassia, betel nuts, and others. All these valuable products, combined with valuable timber in the forests, such as teak and so on, are a testimony to the fertility of the soil and the richness of the land. Of late years the coffee shrub has been successfully cultivated in all the hilly districts, bringing capital into the country, enriching the people, and laying the foundation of much future prosperity.

The history of the connection of Travancore with the British Government need not be entered upon here. The province has undoubtedly derived the greatest benefits from the long intercourse of fifty or sixty years with the European world, and the naturally quiet disposition of the people has been as instrumental as anything else in leading them to enjoy and appreciate the blessings of peace. The rapid spread of education among all classes, so energetically fostered by the enlightened minister, Sir Madava Rao, when Dewan of the country, has tended to sweep away many prejudices and open the paths of civilisation to a people eminently fitted for advancement. With every advantage for communication with foreign countries, the march of improvement must steadily progress in this beautiful land, and a faithful alliance with the British Government must be productive of that increasing wealth and prosperity it so richly deserves.